Table of Figures

Dedication

This book is dedicated to our partners and families. We thank them for their support through the years.

Book published by BookSurge Publishing, New York, 2004.

ISBN: 1-59457-667-X

Preface

Steganography is a process which involves hiding a message in an appropriate carrier for example an image or an audio file. The carrier can then be sent to a receiver without anyone else knowing that it contains a hidden message. This is a process which can be used for example by civil rights organisations in repressive states to communicate their message to the outside world without their own government being aware of it. Less virtuously it can be used by terrorists to communicate with one another without anyone else's knowledge. In both cases the objective is not to make it difficult to read the message as cryptography does, it is to hide the existence of the message in the first place possibly to protect the courier.

The aim of this book is to investigate steganography and how it is implemented. Based on information provided in this work, a number of common methods of steganography should then be implementable. This book is aimed at under-graduate students working in the field of image analysis, cryptography and steganography. The free java software provided with the book allows users to evaluate the effectiveness of many of the algorithms outlined.

The software can be downloaded for free at http://www.infm.ulst.ac.uk/~kevin/steganography.zip.

Outline of the Book

This Book is divided into 8 chapters. Chapter 1 introduces the subject. It reviews steganography in general and steganography for images in particular. Chapter 2 looks at common steganography digital image software that exists at present. Some steganography methods are also introduced here. Chapter 3 investigates steganalysis. Chapter 4 describes watermarking while chapter 5 introduces the area of cryptography. Chapter 6 describes in detail some of the more common steganography methodologies and chapter 7 introduces the Chameleon steganography software and presents a walkthrough of using the free software to encrypt and decrypt images. Chapter 8 provides a conclusion to the book followed by a list of references.

1 Steganography Introduction

This chapter presents an overview of the steganography process, different steganographic methods, and steganalysis methods. It also briefly looks at related issues such as watermarking and cryptography.

The word steganography means "covered or hidden writing" (Johnson et al, 2001). The object of steganography is to send a message through some innocuous carrier (Johnson et al, 2001) to a receiver while preventing anyone else from knowing that a message is being sent at all.

> "the art of passing information in a manner that the very existence of the message is unknown."

> "to avoid drawing suspicion to the transmission of a hidden message."
> (Johnson and Jajodia, 1998)

Computer based stenography allows changes to be made to what are known as digital carriers such as images or sounds. The changes represent the hidden message, but result if successful in no discernible change to the carrier. The information may be nothing to do with the carrier sound or image or it might be information about the carrier such as the author or a digital watermark or fingerprint (Johnson et al, 2001). Cryptography and steganography are different. Cryptographic techniques can be used to scramble a message so that if it is discovered it cannot be read. If a cryptographic message is discovered it is generally known to be a piece of hidden information (anyone intercepting it will be suspicious) but it is scrambled so that it is difficult or impossible to understand and de-code. Steganography hides the very existence of a message so that if successful it generally attracts no suspicion at all (Johnson et al, 2001). Using steganography, information can be hidden in carriers such as images, audio files, text files, videos and data transmissions (Johnson et al, 2001). When the message is hidden in the carrier a stego-carrier is formed for example a stego-image. Hopefully it will be perceived to be as close as possible to the original carrier or cover image by the human senses.

Images are the most widespread carrier medium (Westfield and Pfitzmann, 1999). They are used for steganography in the following way. The message may firstly be encrypted. The sender (or embedder (Pfitzmann, 1996)) embeds the secret message to be sent into a graphic file (Zollner et al, 1998) (the cover image (Pfitzmann, 1996) or the carrier). This results in the production of what is called a stego-image. Additional secret data may be needed in the hiding process e.g. a stegokey (Pfitzmann, 1996). The stego-image is then transmitted to the recipient (Zollner et al, 1998). The recipient (or extractor (Pfitzmann, 1996)) extracts the message from the carrier image. The message can only be extracted if there is a shared secret between the sender and the recipient. This could be the algorithm for extraction or a special parameter such as a key (Zollner et al, 1998) (the stegokey). A stegoanalyst or attacker may try to intercept the stego-image. Figure 1 below shows the steganographic system.

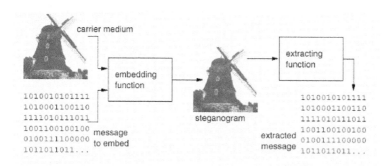

Figure 1: The Steganographic System (Westfield/Pfitzmann, 99)

To make a steganographic communication even more secure the message can be compressed and encrypted before being hidden in the carrier. Cryptography and steganography can be used together. If compressed the message will take up far less space in the carrier and will minimise the information to be sent. The random looking message which would result from encryption and compression would also be easier to hide than a message with a high degree of regularity (Fridrich, 1999). Therefore encryption and compression are recommended in conjunction with steganography (Fridrich, 1999).

1.1 Types of Digital Carriers

There are a variety of digital carriers or places where data can be hidden. Data may be embedded in files at imperceptible levels as noise (Johnson et al, 2001). Properties of images can be manipulated including luminescence, contrast and colours (Johnson et al, 2001). In audio files small echoes or slight delays can be included or subtle signals can be masked with sounds of higher amplitude (Johnson et al, 2001). Information can be hidden in documents by manipulating the positions of the lines or the words (Johnson et al, 2001). When HTML files are written web browsers ignore spaces, tabs, certain characters and extra line breaks. These could be used as locations in which to hide information. Messages can be retrieved from text by taking for example the second letter of each word and using them to produce the hidden message (Johnson et al, 2001). This is called a null cipher or open code (Johnson et al, 2001). Information can be hidden in the layout of a document for example certain words in a piece of text can be shifted very slightly from their positions and these shifted words can then make up the hidden message. The way a language is spoken can be used to encode a message such as pauses, enunciation's and throat clearing (Johnson et al, 2001).

Unused or reserved space on a disc can be used to hide information (Johnson et al, 2001). The way operating systems store files typically results in unused space that appears to be allocated to the files (Johnson et al, 2001). A minimum amount of space may be allocated to files but the file does not need all this space so some of it goes unused (Johnson et al, 2001). This space can be used to hide information. Another method for hiding information in file systems is to create a hidden partition (Johnson et al, 2001). Data may be hidden in unused space in file headers. Packets for example TCP / IP packets have headers with unused space and other features that can be manipulated to embed information (Johnson et al, 2001). Data can be hidden using the physical arrangement of a carrier for example the layout of code in a program or electronic circuits on a board. This process can be used to record and identify the origin of the design and cannot be removed without a substantial change to the physical layout (Johnson et al, 2001).

Spread spectrum techniques can also be used by placing an audio signal over a number of different frequencies. Random number generators are developed to allow spread spectrum radios to hop from frequency to frequency. Systems can use different frequencies at the same time. Some information is broadcast on one frequency and some on another. The message can be reassembled by combining all the information (Wayner, 2002).

1.2 Image Structure and Image Processing

A digital image is the most common type of carrier used for steganography. A digital image is produced using a camera, scanner or other device. The digital representation is an approximation of the original image (Efford, 2000). The system used for producing the image focuses a two dimensional pattern of varying light intensity and colour onto a sensor (Efford, 2000). The pattern has a co-ordinate system and the origin is the upper left hand corner of the image. The pattern can be described by a function $f(x, y)$. An image can be described as an array of numbers that represent light intensities at various points (Johnson et al, 2001). These light intensities or instances of colour are called pixels.

Sampling is the process of measuring the value of the image function $f(x, y)$ at discrete intervals in space (Efford, 2000). Each sample is the small square area of the image known as the pixel. The raster data of an image is that part of the image that can be seen i.e. the pixels (Johnson et al, 2001). The size of an image can be given in pixels, for example an image which is 640 x 480 pixels contains 307,200 pixels (Johnson et al, 2001). Pixels are indexed by x and y co-ordinates with x and y having integer values (Efford, 2000). The spatial resolution of an image is the physical size of the pixel in the image. Dense sampling produces a high-resolution image in which there are many pixels and each contributes a small part of the scene. Coarse sampling results in a low-resolution image in which there are fewer pixels (Efford, 2000). The rate of change of the value $f(x, y)$ as it moves across the image is the spatial frequency. Gradual changes in $f(x, y)$ correspond to low spatial frequencies and can be represented in a coarsely sampled image. Rapid changes correspond to high spatial frequencies and must be represented by a densely sampled image. The Nyquist criterion states that the sampling frequency should be at least double the highest spatial frequency found in the image. A coarsely sampled image that does not follow this criterion may suffer from the effects of aliasing (Efford, 2000) shown in Figure 2 below.

a.   b.

Figure 2: Aliasing Artefacts in Digital Images

Each pixel is generally stored as 24-bit or 8-bit. A 24-bit pixel has a possibility of 2^{24} colour combinations (Johnson et al, 2001). The 24 bits of a 24-bit image are spread over three bytes and each byte represents red, green and blue respectively. Colours are obtained by mixing red, green and blue light in different proportions (Efford, 2000). An image can be formed by making three measurements of brightness at each pixel using the red, green and blue components of the detected light. Using the RGB model the value of f(x, y) is a vector with three components corresponding to red (R), green (G) and blue (B). They can be regarded as orthogonal axes defining a three dimensional colour space. Every value of f(x, y) is a point in the colour cube shown in Figure 3 below. The three components are normally quantised using 8 bits. An image made of these components is described as a 24-bit colour image (Efford, 2000).

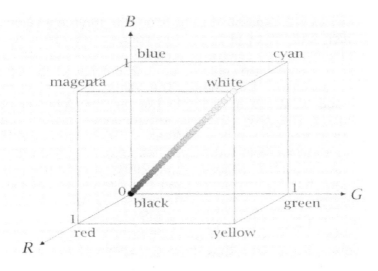

Figure 3: The RGB Colour Cube (Efford, 2000)

Each byte can have a value from 0 to 255 representing the intensity of the colour. The darkest colour value is 0 and the brightest is 255. For example a pixel could be made up of three bytes as follows: 11111111 00000000 00000000. The first 8 bits represent red, the second 8 bits represent green and the third 8 bits represent blue. The bit values in this example result in a red pixel. Its red byte is at a maximum value (11111111) and its green (00000000) and blue (00000000) bytes have the lowest possible value.

Transparency is controlled by the addition of information to each element of the pixel data. This is to allow image overlay (Murray and van Ryper, 1996). A 24-bit pixel value can be stored in 32 bits. The extra 8 bits specify transparency. This is sometimes called the alpha channel (Murray and van Ryper, 1996). An ideal 8-bit alpha channel can support transparency levels from 0 (completely transparent) to 255 (completely opaque). It can be stored as part of the pixel data (Murray and van Ryper, 1996) e.g. RGBA (red, green, blue and alpha taking up 4 bytes in total).

Some images are 8-bit. Each pixel is represented by one byte only. This one byte can have any value ranging from

0 to 255, 256 possible colours or 256 greyscale values for black and white images. The colours are taken from a colour index or palette also called a colour map or colour table. This palette contains up to 256 colours representing the colours in the image. The value of the pixel in an image points to a colour in the palette (Johnson et al, 2001). The GIF (Graphic Interchange Format) image format uses this process. When a GIF image is displayed the software paints the specified colour from the palette onto the screen (Johnson et al, 2001) at each pixel. If the image has fewer colours than the size of the palette any unused colours in the palette are set to zero (Murray and van Ryper, 1996). GIF is a bitmap image. Bitmap is a system in which an image is described as a bit pattern or series of numbers that gives the shade or colour of each pixel (Day, 1998). In true greyscale images, values from 0 to 255 represent the intensity of the colour and do not refer to a palette (Johnson et al, 2001). A palette image format contains a header, a palette and image data (pointers to the palette).

There are two steps in creating palette-based images - colour quantisation and dithering (Fridrich, 1999). A colour quantisation algorithm has two parts, generating the colour palette and mapping the pixels. To generate the palette colours are extracted from the image. Each pixel in the image is then mapped to its nearest colour in the palette to generate the quantized image (Hsieh and Fan, 1999). Quantisation involves replacing a continuously varying f(x, y) with a set of quantisation levels (Efford, 2000). A set of quantisation levels comprises the integers 0, 1,2,3... n-1. 0 and n-1 are displayed as black and white with intermediate levels in shades of grey (greyscale). The number of grey levels is usually an integral power of 2.

$$n = 2^b$$

b is the number of bits used for quantisation. It is typically 8 resulting in images with 256 grey levels ranging from black to white (Efford, 2000).

There are different algorithms for quantisation. Colour quantisation involves truncating all the colours of the original 24-bit image to a finite number of colours, 256 for GIF, 216 for Netscape GIF and 2 for black and white. Splitting algorithms split the colour space of the original image into two subspaces according to some preference criteria (Hsieh and Fan, 1999). The splitting is iteratively carried out until the correct number of subspaces is reached. The colour representing the subspace becomes the quantized colour. Clustering methods can also be used in which colours are clustered to form the quantized colours (Hsieh and Fan, 1999). The method usually used for quantization involves iterative dividing of a three dimensional colour cube into two boxes with approximately the same number of colours. The half with the largest dimensions is chosen by measuring either the greatest difference in RGB value or the greatest difference in luminosity (Wayner, 2002). The half with the largest dimensions is selected and the iteration is continued until the desired number of colours is produced (Fridrich, 1999). The centres of gravity of each box are then rounded to integer colours representing the colours of the palette. The largest dimension can be replaced using the largest standard deviation resulting in a slightly better algorithm (Fridrich, 1999). It should be noted that standard quantisation algorithms will not necessarily yield exactly 256 colours in he image.

Dithering is a technique used to simulate colours that are missing from an images palette. This is done by intermingling pixels of two or more palette colours. Colours are reordered so that their visual combination matches the original images more closely (Lemstrom and Franti, 1999). If the unavailable colour differs too much from the colours in the palette a grainy appearance results (Johnson et al, 2001) and errors are present in the form of false contours (Lemstrom and Franti, 1999).

Dithering can be based on error diffusion. The image is scanned in some regular way for example by rows. The colour of a pixel is rounded to its closest colour in the palette. This produces an error. The error is negative if the rounding has resulted in a decrease in the pixel value.

The error is positive if the rounding has increased the pixel value. The error is multiplied by weights and added to the surrounding pixels that have not yet been visited. Using this method the rounding error is spread to neighbouring pixels which results in an image that is more visually pleasing (Fridrich, 1999). This process is repeated for every colour in the image (Johnson et al, 2001).

1.3 File Compression

There are two types of compression lossless and lossy (Kurak and McHugh, 1992). Some file types are compressed using lossy methods which results in the loss of certain data and the reconstruction of an image that is similar but not exactly the same as the original. The advantage of lossless compression is that the original image is reproduced exactly and therefore the original arrangement of bits making up the image is maintained. Lossless compression rarely achieves as high a compression rate as lossy compression. GIF and 8-bit BMP image formats use a lossless process of compression.

GIF files use Lempel-Ziv-Welch (LZW) compression (Stevens, 1999). Strings of identical byte values are converted into a single code word reducing pixel data by 40% or more (Murray and van Ryper, 1996). LZW uses a table of character strings and a code is assigned to each string. The codes are then stored instead of the character string. The table is created while the image is scanned. The table itself does not need to be saved but can be recreated from the stored compressed data and used to create the original image (Stevens, 1999). The LZW technique must normally be paid for however the software is included in Java so that working on GIF programs in Java does not require any payment (Stevens, 1999).

Images saved in JPEG use lossy compression in which the image is not reconstructed in exactly the same way as the original. Space is saved in storing the image however some of the bits and hence some of the data will be lost for example some of the background detail. DCT (Discrete Cosine Transform) is the name of the algorithm used to compress JPEG images. The compressed information is stored as integers (Johnson and Jajodia, 1998).

1.4 Application of Steganography to Images

When images are used as the carrier in steganography they are generally manipulated by changing one or more of the bits of the byte or bytes that make up the pixels of an image. The least significant bit (LSB) of a byte may be used to encode the bits of the message e.g. a messages characters can be converted to bytes in binary form using ASCII code and then each bit of this binary list of bytes can be stored a bit at a time in a series of pixels. Generally the LSB for a colour byte is first identified. If it corresponds to the bit which needs to be embedded it is left unchanged. Otherwise it is changed to correspond to the bit being hidden. These LSBs can then be read by the recipient of the stegoed image and put together as bytes in order to reproduce the hidden message. The reason the LSB is the bit in the byte that is manipulated is due to the fact that changing the LSB will only change the value of the byte by one. This will not noticeable alter the visual appearance of a colour. Changing a more significant bit may cause a proportionately greater change in the visual appearance of a colour.

Figure 4a below shows a black and white digital image which is busy and contains noise. Below in Figure 4b is the same image but displaying only the LSBs. The most significant bits have been deleted showing a high level of randomness. However in a less busy image the least significant bits can display a very rough indication of the contents of the image. Figure 4c shows the most significant bits of the image. The 7 least significant bits have been deleted.

A carrier image contains randomness such as noise. This is as a result of digitisation. It is the existence of this noise that allows some changes to be made to the image. It is hoped that artefacts created by steganography will simply be viewed as normal noise (Westfield and Pfitzmann, 1999).

a.

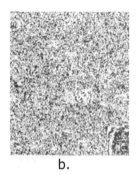

b.

c.

Figure 4: a. A Digital Black and White Image b. The Least Significant Bits of the Image and c. the Most Significant Bits of the Image (Wayner, 2002)

Image modelling describes the areas of images that can be manipulated in order to hide information (Johnson et al, 2001). There are four basic components of the model: image noise, texture, clutter (scene noise) and signal (Rosenfeld, 1992). Embedding in the least significant bits of images is categorised under image noise. Texture can be manipulated by changing the texture of some background surfaces in the image (Johnson et al, 2001). In this way an owner can mark the image (using a Watermark). Clutter refers to small objects being placed into the image. Another method of hiding information in an image would be to change the lowest or medium frequency coefficients of a DCT of an image (Cox et al, 1996).

The location of the message in the image can vary. The message may be spread evenly over the entire image or may be introduced into areas where it may be difficult to detect a small change such as a busy area of the image (Johnson et al, 2001). A busy area is also known as an area of high frequency. This is an area in which there are considerable changes in colour intensity over a small area of the image. It is also an area to which the human eye is relatively insensitive (Fridrich, 1999). However the high frequency areas of an image are those most likely to be lost during lossy compression. A message could be repeated over the image multiple times in a type of pattern. In this way if any part of the image is lost or cropped the message can still be read. A pseudo random number generator could be used to choose random pixels or areas (Johnson et al, 2001) in which to embed the message (Fridrich, 1999). The longer the message is the more it will modify the carrier and the easier it will be to detect (Fridrich, 1999).

In a 24-bit image the LSB of each of the three bytes could be used to store a total of 3 bits of message data (Johnson et al, 2001). Therefore a 1024 x 768 bit image could hold 2,359,296 bits of data (Johnson et al, 2001). Alternatively the LSB of only one of the three bytes could be used to store the message bit. Thus a 1024 x 768 bit image could hold 786,432 bits of data. The data hiding capacity is reduced by two-thirds but the distortion to the image is also reduced as well as the number of new colours created.

There are two ways of hiding messages in palette-based images: embedding the message in the palette or embedding the message into the image pixels. Palette based images are limited in the number of colours available i.e. the number of colours contained in the palette. Therefore embedding the message in the palette is limited by the size of the palette (Fridrich, 1999). Using the image data for embedding is less restrictive on capacity than hiding data in the palette. Practical methods should allow for the use of the full image size, thus the amount of data that can be hidden is proportionate to the number of pixels in the image rather than to the palette size (Fridrich, 1999). Embedding into an image will result in the production of new colours. The palette must be able to cope with these new colours. If the palette is created which contains 128 colours this will allow for the creation of a new colour for every existing colour in the palette. The only restriction is then the size of the image.

The least significant bit does not have to be the bit used to store the information (Wayner, 2002). It could be any of the bits as long as the palette consisted of pairs of similar colours differing by that bit (Wayner, 2002). This process might make it harder to determine the existence of a message (Wayner, 2002) (harder to determine patterns) if the hacker is looking for the message in the least significant bit, which is the more typical steganographic process. Another possibility for storing information might be to use more than one bit in each byte (Wayner, 2002). If the colour depth of the image is decreased to 64 or 32 this allows for more new colours to be produced as a result of adjustment of the LSB and/or 2nd and/or 3rd LSB (Fridrich, 1999). The algorithm which was used to determine 256 or 128 colours could be used to determine the 64 or 32 colours that best represent the image (Wayner, 2002). One two or three bits per pixel can, in certain cases, be embedded without visible change to the image (Fridrich, 1999). For example if the palette was reduced to 64 colours 6 bits per pixel could represent the 64 colours and the other 2 could be used to hide information (Wayner, 2002). These two bits also allow for four very similar versions of each of the 64 colours. This does result however in less initial colour being available to represent the image and hence a degraded image (Wayner, 2002). If the palette is reduced to 32 colours three bits per pixel can be hidden while still not creating so many new colours that they exceed the palette size of 256. If 4 bits were used to represent the colour then there would be only 16 colours, 4 bits in which to store the message and 16 versions of each colour (Wayner, 2002). The problem with this is that it will result in the new palette having groups of similar colours and therefore it might be easier to detect and consequently conclude that the image is likely to contain a message (Fridrich, 1999). Although the colours are very restricted an area of one particular colour in the image may have 16 variations distributed through it which could result in a certain amount of texture mitigating the effects of such a restricted palette (Wayner, 2002). The difference in the 16 variations may be to some extent perceptible. Even though the colours in the original palette have been reduced the steganography process will create new colours which will to some extent make up for colours lost especially when examining the palette. Greyscale palettes are particularly useful in this case because of the gradual changes of the 256 shades of grey (Johnson et al, 2001).

Changing the LSB of the numbers representing the palette colours will change the pointer or index to point to another colour in the palette. One method of steganography for example embeds one message bit into each pixel which is in reality the pointer to the palette containing a colour value for that pixel (Fridrich, 1999). However the colour which the new pointer is pointing to may be noticeably different from the original. This could result in the new pixel colour standing out very obviously from the pixels around it in the image creating noise or excessive degradation of the image (Johnson et al, 2001). The palette will display for example dark red, medium red and light red however beside light red could be a light sienna. Therefore if information were hidden in the least significant bit of the pixel byte representing the index the pixel might for example be light red. It may also be part of a large continuous area of light red. The result displayed in the stego-image could be either medium red which wouldn't be too noticeable or light sienna which would be quite noticeable and would result in a patchy noisy non continuous area of red. This would result in a suspicious looking image. For this reason one method of steganography EzStego involves ordering the palette by luminance. The algorithm finds the closest colour with the desired parity to the colour of the current pixel (in which a message bit is to be embedded) measured by luminance. However colours with similar luminance values are occasionally relatively far from each other i.e. they can be very different colours.

There are solutions to this problem. One of the methods typically used is to half the number of colours down to 128 as mentioned above but following this a second 128 colours are chosen which are extremely similar to the first 128. The similar colours would differ only by their least significant bit. Therefore if the value 1 was to be hidden in a particular pixel the closest colour to it in the new palette would be found. Two very similar colours would represent this colour and the one with the LSB set to 1 would be chosen (Wayner, 2002). Another possibility is to determine the closest colour by distance with a different parity bit to all the colours in the palette. When a colour is replaced by its closest colour with the correct parity bit is will be relatively close to the original colour. An advantage of this method is also that it results in no changes to the palette itself (Fridrich, 1999). These methods were used by different authors and will be explained further below.

Another possible method of steganography would be to hide encrypted messages in the least significant bits of the palette colours. The perturbed palette however must still be consistent with the noise model of the original image. This could be carried out in each case by studying the sensitivity of the colour quantisation process to perturbations. However if the palette is later reordered it may be difficult to remove the message from the LSBs of the palette entries. The order of the palette will change after a message has been embedded. The palette must be initially analysed before a message is embedded to find what palette entries can be changed without disturbing the palette order. One possibility would be to embed a single bit into each palette entry. This would further decrease the already limited capacity of the palette (Fridrich, 1999).

Another way of storing a message is to permute the palette instead of the colours of the image using for example a process called Gifshuffle (Kwan, 1998). This involves moving the colours in the palette into a very specific order relating to the message to be stored. The appearance of the image will not be adjusted which is an advantage for security however image processing software may later order the palette by luminance or frequency of occurrence or other scalar factor which would be a security risk. Also if the palette is randomised it may look suspicious. Further if the image is opened and displayed and then resaved the software used may rewrite and reorder the palette. The palette also has an extremely limited capacity (Fridrich, 1999).

Bits of information can also be inserted into coefficients of image transforms such as Fourier Transform or Discrete Cosine Transform. These techniques are more robust with regard to common image processing operations and lossy compression (Fridrich, 1999). The DCT (Discrete Cosine Transform) and FFT (Fast Fourier Transform) are in a particular class of mathematical operations. The basic operation is to take a signal and transform it from one type of representation to another (Nelson, 1992).

Digital audio signals can be analysed using FFT. When a set of sample points is collected for an incoming audio signal a representation of a signal in the time domain can be produced. Therefore the set of points show what the voltage level (amplitude) was for the input signal at each point in time. FFT transforms the sample points into a set of frequency values that describe exactly the same signal. Figure 5 below shows an analog signal. It is made up of three different sine waves added together to form a more complex waveform (Nelson, 1992). The x-axis represents a point in time. The y-axis represents the magnitude of the signal. Figure 6 shows the same set of points after FFT processing. Each point of the x-axis now represents a specific frequency and the y-axis specifies the magnitude of the frequency (Nelson, 1992). The process is reversible from the second representation back to the first.

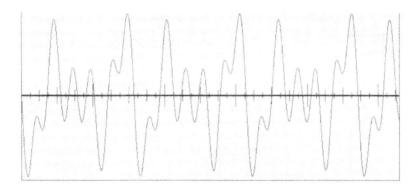

Figure 5: Classic Time Domain Representation of an Analog Signal

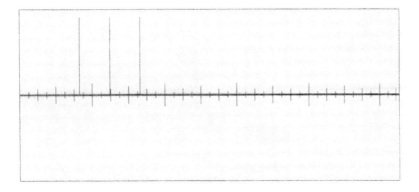

Figure 6: Data Points after FFT Processing

An image can also be represented in the frequency domain as well as in the spatial domain (Efford, 2000). As was mentioned earlier the rate of change of the value f(x, y) as it moves across the image is the spatial frequency. Spatial frequency can be described as the areas of an image in which the grey level varies rapidly (Efford, 2000). Fourier developed the idea that a periodic function even if it is quite complex can be represented as a sum of simpler sinusoidal functions (Efford, 2000). He developed a way in which functions could be modelled using a set of sine and cosine functions (Wayner, 2002). The idea is to take a function and represent it as a weighted sum of a group of other functions. This is useful for steganography as it means that several signals could be embedded together into a larger one. An image can be broken down into a set of sinusoidal components or waves with particular frequencies.

The different frequencies can be overlaid to produce the image and the frequency coefficients can be used to determine how much of a particular frequency is present. The amplitude of the wave represents the size of variation in grey level or the value of the pixel at a point in the image (Nelson, 1992), (Efford, 2000). The image can be represented in a two-dimensional way also with waves going in both the x and y directions. For any spatial frequency it can be determined how much of a particular frequency is present in the image.

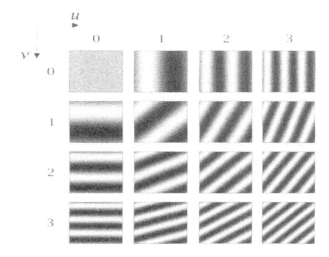

Figure 7: Some of the Basis Images used in a Fourier Representation of an Image (Efford, 2000)

FFT separates the frequencies of an image into rings centred around an x and y axis. Those rings closest to the axis represent the low frequencies of the image, and those furthest away represent the high frequencies. This is shown in Figure 7. In the frequency domain encoding method, the secret message is encoded in the middle frequencies of the image. This is done by converting the message text to bits and overlaying these bits in a ring shape in the desired frequency band on the 2-D FFT. Although the ring of bits appears dark and outstanding on the 2-D FFT, the effect on the image itself is very slight. Also, an image encoded by this method is able to better withstand noise, compression, translation, and rotation, than images encoded by the LSB method.

The DCT takes a set of points from the spatial domain and transforms them into a representation in the frequency domain. However instead of a two-dimensional signal the DCT operates on a 3D signal plotted on a x, y and z-axis. In this situation the signal is a graphical image. A graphical image can be looked at as a three dimensional signal. The x and y axis are the two dimensions of the screen. The x and y axis represent the frequencies of the signal in two different dimensions. The amplitude in this case is the value of a pixel at a point on the screen (Nelson, 1992). The value on the z axis is a colour on the screen at a given point (Nelson, 1992). This is the spatial representation of the signal or image. The frequency representation can be converted back to a spatial one. The DCT is performed on an N x N square matrix of pixel values and it yields an N x N square matrix of frequency coefficients. In the matrix all the elements in row 0 have a frequency component of zero in one direction of the signal and all elements in column 0 have a frequency component of zero in the other direction. Moving away from the origin the coefficients in the transformed matrix represent higher frequencies. This is shown in Figure 8.

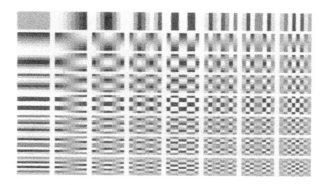

Figure 8: The 64 Different 2D Basis Functions used in the 2D Discrete Cosine Transform of an 8 x 8 Grid of Pixels (Wayner, 2002)

Most graphical images are composed of low frequency information and this information is more useful than the high frequency information. Therefore the higher frequency information can afford to be lost during lossy compression. It has been suggested therefore that the most significant parts of the image is the most desirable place to hide information as it is less likely to be lost during compression. Information is added by modifying the frequencies and recreating the image matrix from the frequency matrix (Wayner, 2002). DCT is used in JPEG format to achieve image compression (Johnson and Jajodia, 1998).

Modifications to the image can be reduced by embedding one message bit into clusters of pixels. The image is divided into clusters of random pixels and the message bit is encoded as a parity of the sum of all the pixel parities (Fridrich and Du, 1999).

Adaptive steganography adapts the message embedding technique to the actual content and features of the image. An example of this is avoiding areas of uniform colour and selecting pixels with large local standard deviation. To carry out this process the image is divided into disjoint blocks (e.g. 3X3 blocks) (Fridrich and Du, 1999). At most one bit is to be assigned to each block. A threshold for the local standard deviation is selected. A secret key generates a pseudo random non-intersecting walk over the blocks. If the local standard deviation of a block is above the threshold and stays above it after embedding, that block is used for message embedding. If it falls below after message embedding the change is made but the block is not included for message embedding and the same bit is carried on to the next block. Local standard deviation could be replaced for example with the number of colours in the block. For low colour images this process works better (Murray and van Ryper, 1996). Any pixel in the block could be modified which leads to smaller modifications of the image. A problem is that it is impossible to determine whether or not a message of a certain length will fit into the image before embedding begins. Capacity is also decreased by this process (Murray and van Ryper, 1996).

1.5   Image Formats

There are several different types of image file formats that can be used for steganography and each has certain advantages and disadvantages for hiding messages. There are two types of images on the Internet available in a palette format GIF and PNG (Fridrich, 1999). GIF will be looked at in some detail.

1.5.1   GIF

GIF (Graphics Interchange Format) is used for the purpose of storing multiple bitmap images in a single file for exchange between platforms and images (Murray and van Ryper, 1996). It is often used for storing multibit graphics and image data. GIF is not associated with a particular software application but was designed "to allow the easy interchange and viewing of image data stored on local or remote computer systems" (Murray and van Ryper, 1996). GIF is stream based and is made up of a series of data packets called blocks (which can be found anywhere in the file) and protocol information. GIF files are read as a continuous stream of data and the screen is read pixel by pixel (Stevens, 1999).

Data block categories (Murray and van Ryper, 1996):

1. Graphics Control Extension block – a graphics control block
2. Plain Text Extension Blocks - Graphics rendering block
3. Local Image Descriptor – Graphics rendering block
4. Image Data Block – bitmap data
5. Comment Extension blocks - special purpose blocks
6. Application Extension Blocks – special purpose blocks

Blocks store fields of information and contain sub blocks. The GIF format stores image data as a series of data sub blocks (Murray and van Ryper, 1996). Each sub block starts with a single count byte in the range of 1 to 255 which gives the number of data bytes following the count byte. It is followed by a group of data blocks. Sub blocks may occur as follows: Count byte, data bytes, count byte, data bytes etc. The sequence ends with a count byte which has a value of zero (Murray and van Ryper, 1996). The original version of GIF was GIF87a (Murray and van Ryper, 1996) and the most recent version is GIF89a.

GIF can store many images in one file but although this is now supported by many GIF file viewers it is recommended that one image per file is stored (Murray and van Ryper, 1996). Each GIF file begins with a Header and a Logical Screen Descriptor. It may also contain a Global Colour Table. Each image stored in the file contains a Local Image Descriptor, an optional Local Colour Table and a block of image data. A Local Colour Table may or may not be present (Murray and van Ryper, 1996). The Colour Table entries can be sorted from the most frequently occurring colour in the image to the least important however the table may or may not be sorted (Day, 1998). The Global Colour Table is the colour map used to index the pixel colour data contained within the image data. The Local Colour Table is used for each image if there are multiple images in the file. The application may supply a Default Colour Table if a Local Colour or Global Colour Table is not present (Murray and van Ryper, 1996). The Global Colour Table is a series of three byte triples making up the elements of the table. Each triple contains the red, green and blue primary colour values for each entry in the table. The number of entries in the table is always to the power of 2 up to a maximum of 256 (Murray and van Ryper, 1996).

Each sub block must be read and the data sent to an LZW encoder (Day, 1998). The format for the decoded GIF image data contains each pixel in a decoded scan line which is one byte in size containing an index value to the colour table. GIF image data is always stored by scan line and pixel. They may be stored in consecutive order starting with the first row or they can be interlaced which means the image is stored as alternating rows of bitmap data. If an interlaced image was appearing on a screen when the down load was 50% complete the entire image could be discerned and the viewers brain could fill in the missing information (Day, 1998).

Most GIF files contain 16 colour or 256 colour images. The pixels may be in colour or greyscale but GIF is not usually used for monochrome graphics such as Clipart (Murray and van Ryper, 1996). In GIF format the colour of each of the images pixels is displayed as the closest possible colour taken from a palette of colours in the table. The image displayed may not be an absolutely true representation of the colours in the original scanned image.

1.5.2 JPEG

Joint Photographic Experts Group (JPEG) was set up to create a set of standards for transmitting digital graphic and image data (Stevens, 1999). Colours are represented by between 6 and 24 bits (Stevens, 1999). JPEG is not made up of one single algorithm but a collection of compression methods. JPEG is a standard compression method for compressing photographs. JPEG is compressed using lossy compression. If a file compressed with JPEG is uncompressed it will look similar but not exactly the same as the original (Wayner, 2002). The amount of detail lost depends on the level of compression used. It represents areas of similar colour by just one colour and can therefore be used where there are large blocks of the same colour in an image. Two methods are run length compression and block compression. Lossy compression will result in fraying around the edges of objects.

1.6 Hiding the Sender

There are various ways in which to minimise the likelihood of a message being found. If an image containing a message is located on the senders web page then anyone who discovers the message will know who it came from (Wayner, 2002). A way of preventing this happening is to spread the message out over a number of images located on different web sites (Wayner, 2002). In this way it will be impossible to know who sent the information (Wayner, 2002). It may be the author of one of the sites but it may not be. If a message is split up into several parts and each part located in a different image on a different web site only the person who is supposed to receive the message will know which images to collect (Wayner, 2002). When collected the files could then be XORed together to reveal the message. Using this method no one knows where the information came from possibly not ever the intended receiver. In order to carry out this type of steganography the sender could go into various web sites, hack into an image, carry out steganography on the image and leave the stego-image on the site. However if this is done the adjusted image on the web site will have a much newer creation date that the rest of the site. Therefore it would be necessary to adjust the date so that it is the same as the rest of the site. HTTP however does not normally send this type of information to web browsers (Wayner, 2002). To avoid problems with identifying a new date the clock on the PC can be reset (Wayner, 2002).

The other problem with changing images on foreign web sites is that the image will end up having a different structure to the other images on the same site (Wayner, 2002). It is better therefore to choose an image which has the right structure in the first place. Error correcting features could also be used to store messages (Wayner, 2002). Three different sets of images could be used. When they are compared by the receiver three different sets of hidden bits would be found. The correct bits would be the ones found to be the same in two out of three of the images (Wayner, 2002). An error correcting code could be used that converts every 8 bits into a 12-bit block which can be used to recover errors. One bit from each of the 12-bit blocks could be put into 12 different files and these files could be hidden in 12 different images on different parts of the network (Wayner, 2002). The receiver may not be able to recover all 12 images but the error correcting code would still allow the receiver to retrieve the message (Wayner, 2002).

A suitable image and in the case of palette based images a suitable palette needs to be chosen for addition of a piece of data by steganography. The best types of images to use are black and white greyscale (Wayner, 2002) or natural photographs with 24 bits per pixel (Zollner et al 1998) which have been scanned in (Wohlgemuth, 2002). The redundancy of the data helps to hide the presence of a secret message (Fridrich and Du, 1999). The cover image should contain some randomness. It should contain some natural uncertainty or noise (Johnson et al, 2001). Once it has been used the image should not be used again and should be destroyed (Wohlgemuth, 2002). The palette image format GIF is recognised by all browsers and used widely over the internet (Fridrich and Du, 1999). It raises less suspicion than for example a BMP format (Fridrich and Du, 1999). Games are excellent places to hide information due to their complex images and textures (Wayner, 2002).

2 Steganography Software

What follows is a description of some of the more common steganography packages.

2.1 Hide and Seek

Hide and Seek is one of the older methods of steganography (Wayner, 2002). Version 4.1 was designed for the PC and written by an author identified by the email address shaggy@phantom.com (Wayner, 2002). The Hide and Seek program displays the image before any data has been added or the message has been extracted. The source code is included with Hide and Seek (Wayner, 2002).

Hide and Seek 4.1 can be used on 8-bit colour or 8-bit black and white GIF files that are 320 by 480 pixels in size (the standard size of the oldest GIF format) (Wayner, 2002). There are 19200 (320*480/8) bytes of space available in this GIF image (Wayner, 2002). In version 4.1 if the cover image is larger than allowed the stego-image is cropped or cut to fit the required size (Johnson et al, 2001). When an image contains a message it should not be resized because if it has to be reduced part of the message bits will be lost. If the image is too small it is padded with black space. There is also a version 5.0. It will work with a wider range of image sizes. However this version of Hide and Seek also uses a restricted range of image sizes. The images must fit to one of these sizes exactly, they are (320 x 200, 320 x 400, 320 x 480, 640 x 400 and 1024 x 768) (Johnson et al, 2001). In version 5 if the image exceeds the maximum allowed which is 1024 x 768 an error message is returned. If the image is smaller than the minimum size necessary the image containing the message is padded out with black space. The padded areas are added before the message is embedded and are therefore also used as areas in which to hide the message (Johnson et al, 2001). But if the padded area is removed the message cannot be recovered fully. These characteristics of Hide and Seek stego-images lead searchers/crackers to the fact that a hidden message exists. Hide and Seek 1.0 for Windows 95 has no size limit restrictions and uses an improved technique for information hiding however it can still only be used on 8-bit images with 256 colours or greyscale (Johnson et al, 2001). BMP images are used with this version instead of GIF images because of licensing issues with GIF image compression (Johnson et al, 2001).

Steganography by this method is carried out by taking the low order bit of each pixel and using it to encode one bit of a character (Maroney). It creates some noise in the image unless a greyscale image is used. The greyscale image creates no noise because of the way the greyscale palette works. When using Hide and Seek with colour GIFs noise is very obvious (Maroney). The greyscale GIFs do not display any of the artefacts or bad image effects associated with 8-bit colour images which have undergone steganography (Wayner, 2002).

The Hide and Seek software currently available contains two programs which help the user in hiding information in GIF files: grey.exe converts colour GIFs into greyscale GIFs. reduce.exe reduces the 256 colour palette to 128 colours and then duplicates the 128 colours. This is done so that entries beside each other in the colour palette are either duplicates of each other (Wayner, 2002) or are extremely similar to one another, so similar that they are not generally visible to the naked eye. When this has been carried out hiding information in the least significant bit won't affect the final appearance of the image (Wayner, 2002).

One of the programs for reducing the size of the palette works as follows (Wayner, 2002):

1. Create a two dimensional grid containing the distances between all the pairs of colours in the palette.

    The distance between (R_1, G_1, B_1) and (R_2, G_2, B_2) is calculated as
    $\delta(R_1, G_1, B_1), (R_2, G_2, B_2) = \sqrt{(R_1-R_2)^2 + (G_1-G_2)^2 + (B_1-B_2)^2}$

2. Find the best colour to delete (that is find the colour with the shortest distance from the chosen colour, using the distance measurement above). Delete the closest colour.

3. Repeat this process with the next colour in the palette and continue until the palette has been reduced to the desired size (Wayner, 2002) for example 128 colours.

Because the palette now contains a reduced number of colours it has become suspicious looking to someone who is scanning the images looking for a hidden message that a message has been hidden. A palette containing only 128 different colours is easy to detect automatically. Of course the palette does actually contain 256 colours, however 128 of them are extremely similar to the other 128.

If a small message is to be embedded into the bits of an image a problem may occur whereby the information will be packed into one part of the image for example the top half. Hide and Seek will arrange it so that the message bits will not be beside one another but instead randomly dispersed throughout the image (Wayner, 2002). Hence the noise will also be randomly distributed. It is therefore necessary to know the location of the bits to find the data and hence the message. A user chosen key can be inserted into a pseudo random number generator which will determine random number which indicate bytes in the image where the least significant bit is to be changed (Wayner, 2002). This makes the system more secure because the reader of the message must know the key in order to determine in which bytes the message bits are hidden. The positions in which the message bits are hidden are not in fact random but do follow some sort of pattern. However the code used to produce them must make them look as random as possible so that it will be difficult to determine the pattern of locations. Hide and Seek must remember the seed and the file size (Maroney). To do this it writes a header to the GIf file. The header is encoded using the IDEA algorithm and the key (Maroney).

An 8-byte header on the message controls how the message data is dispersed. The first two bytes indicate the length of the message. The second two are a random number key. The key is chosen at random when the message is inserted into the image. The key is firstly inserted into the random number generator (Wayner, 2002). In Hide and Seek 4.1 there is a built in C code random number generator. A cryptographically secure random number generator could also be used to increase security or IDEA could be used to encrypt the random numbers using a special key. The third pair of bytes is the version of Hide and Seek used. The fourth pair of bytes is used to complete the eight byte block which is necessary for the IDEA cypher (Wayner, 2002). The 8-byte block is encrypted using the IDEA cipher which has an optional key and is then stored in the first 8 bytes of the image. If the key is not known the header information cannot be understood and the dispersion of the data in the image cannot be found.

Stego-images will have different properties depending on the version of Hide and Seek used. In version 4.1 and version 5 all palette entries in 256 colour images are divisible by four for all bit values (Johnson et al, 2001). Greyscale stego-images have 256 triples. They range in sets of four triples from 0 to 252 with incremental steps of 4 (0, 4, 8,…, 248, 252). This can be detected by looking at the whitish value which is 252 252 252. This signature is unique to Hide and Seek (Johnson et al, 2001), (Johnson and Jajodia, 1998). Later versions of Hide and Seek do not produce the same predictable type of palette patterns as versions 4.1 and 5.0 (Johnson et al, 2001)' (Johnson and Jajodia, 1998).

2.2 EzStego

EzStego is a program written in Java for encoding information in the least significant bits of a GIF image (Wayner, 2002). It was written by Romana Machado who also wrote a program called Stego (Wayner, 2002).

The EzStego program creates a copy of the palette sorted by luminance so that the 256 colours in an 8-bit file flow smoothly from one to the next (Wayner, 2002). Luminance is a linear combination of the three colours red, green and blue (Fridrich, 1999). The palette is sorted by luminance by finding the shortest distance between similar colours. The palette is arranged in such a way as to reduce the occurrence of colours beside each other that contrast too much (Johnson et al, 2001). It works well in greyscale images and also in images which contain related colours (Johnson et al, 2001). The theory for the algorithm is based on the fact that colours close to each other in the luminance ordered palette are close to each other in the colour space (Fridrich, 1999). Two colours with the same luminance however can be very different (Westfield and Pfitzmann, 1999). Two colours for example [6, 98, 233] and [233, 6, 98] have the same luminance but represent two very different colours (Fridrich, 1999).

EzStego sorts the palette by luminance by using the following algorithm (Wayner, 2002): The colours are organised into a list in the following way. Begin with any colour and find another colour in the palette that is most different from it in terms of colour. Insert this second colour into the list and proceed to find a colour in the palette most different from it and so on until the list contains the required number of colours. The problem with this method is that it could result in big gaps in the final palette with too great a jump from one colour to the next (Wayner, 2002).

Luminance is calculated by:

L = (0.299 x red) + (0.587 x green) + (0.114 x blue) (Brown and Shepherd, 1995)

In Figure 9 the order of the colours in the palette is shown. In Figure 9 the colours are shown as sorted by EzStego to follow a shortest path through the RGB cube (Westfield and Pfitzmann, 1999).

If instead of ordering by luminance the program is searched for similar colours it would find it difficult to make the move from a group of similar colours to another group for example from a group of reds to a group of greens (Wayner, 2002).

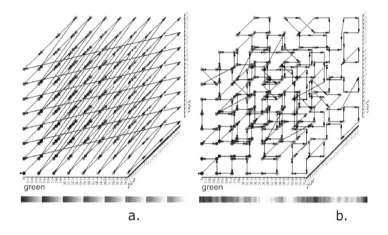

a.   b.

Figure 9: Colour Order in the Palette b. Colours sorted as used by ExStego (Westfield and Pfitzmann, 1999).

The message is then embedded in the LSB of indices pointing to the palette (Fridrich, 1999). Embedding is carried out line by line on an unbroken sequence of pixels from top left to bottom right of the image. After embedding each pixel holds one bit of the message. It is the least significant bit the index would have in the sorted palette (Westfield and Pfitzmann, 1999). Using this process, hidden information that changes the least significant bit of the pointer will only result in small changes to the image (Wayner, 2002). With one-dimensional colour spaces in black and white images this is a trivial process. It is more difficult in three dimensions

(RGB) as the closest colours are not always adjacent (Wayner, 2002).

The Stego part of EzStego is carried out as follows (Fridrich, 1999): The palette has been sorted by luminance. Identify the first pixel in the image. Find the index of that pixel in the sorted palette. Take the first bit from the binary message and replace the LSB of the index as necessary. The index has now been changed. Find the colour that it now points to in the sorted palette. Find the index of this colour in the original unsorted palette. Change the index of the pixel in the image to the index of the new RGB colour from the original palette. Bits are collected from the LSB of the indices in the image file. This procedure would be improved by storing the message bits in randomly selected pixels (Fridrich, 1999).

One of the problems with EzStego is that hiding information may introduce enough visible noise to raise suspicion (Johnson et al, 2001). Therefore the carrier or cover image must be carefully selected.

In order not to raise suspicion about the image the stego-image and the palette can be sent to the receiver unsorted (Wayner, 2002). This is done in the following way. The palette for the image is sorted. The message is encoded in the image and then the palette is unsorted. The image and the unsorted palette are sent to the receiver. The receiver re-sorts the palette using the same algorithm and extracts the message from the image (Wayner, 2002). Therefore en route to the receiver the palette will not raise suspicion.

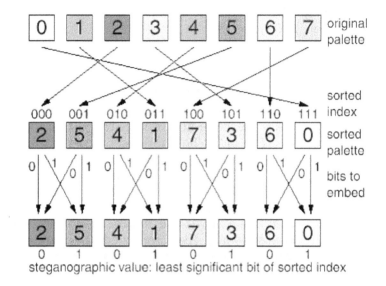

Figure 10: Embedding Function of EzStego (Westfield and Pfitzmann, 1999)

Figure 10 above shows the embedding function of EzStego with a reduced palette. For a chosen pixel in the carrier image index 7 is found. To embed a 1 the index is replaced by 3 and to embed a 0, 7 is left as it is. The colour of index 7 in the original palette is at index 4 in the sorted palette and the colour of index 3 is at index 5 in the sorted palette. The colours are neighbours in the sorted palette and it is hard to distinguish between them (Westfield and Pfitzmann, 1999). The change from 7 to 3 is visually imperceptible unless comparing directly with the original (Westfield and Pfitzmann, 1999). If there is one embedded bit per pixel they can be drawn as an image white for 1 and black for 0 (Westfield and Pfitzmann, 1999).

2.2.1 Fridrichs Method

Another method would be to pair up all the colours in the palette so that the distance between the two colours in each of the pairs is minimized (Wayner, 2002). Instead of sorting the colours in the palette by luminance the algorithm could instead search for the closest colour to the colour of the pixel which has the correct parity for the bit to be hidden (Fridrich, 1999). This is a method which has been proposed by Fridrich.

Fridrichs method involves hiding message bits in the parity bit of the index of close colours. For the colour of each pixel into which a message bit is to be embedded the closest colours in the palette are searched until a palette entry is found with the desired parity bit. This technique does not change the palette (Fridrich, 1999).

The method works as follows: The message is converted into a binary stream of length M. The pixels into which the message is to be stored are randomly chosen using a pseudo random number generator which is seeded with a secret key (Fridrich, 1999). A user-defined seed is used to randomly select M pixels in the image. For each pixel P a set of the closest colours in the palette is calculated by measuring the distance between them. The distance between colours (R_1, G_1, B_1) and (R_2, G_2, B_2) is determined by:

$$\text{square root of } (R_1 - R_2)^2 + (G_1 - G_2)^2 + (B_1 - B_2)^2$$

If the closest colour is the colour of the pixel itself, the next closest colour is selected until a colour is found with the required parity bit. The parity bit of a colour is determined using the calculation R +G + B mod 2 (Fridrich, 1999). Therefore if RGB were as follows: (.......1), (.......0), (.......1) and they were added the parity bit would be 0. The index of the pixel P is then changed to point to the new colour i.e. changed to a new pixel value which is pointing to the nearest colour. Using this method a pixel is never replaced by a completely different colour. To extract the message M pixels are selected using a pseudo random number generator seeded with a user defined seed. The parity bits of the selected pixels are then read and converted back to the message (Fridrich, 1999).

The parity bits of palette entries of real images are randomly distributed therefore using this method it is never necessary to depart from the original colour too much. This avoids the problem of occasionally having to make large changes in colour which might indicate that a message has been hidden (Fridrich, 1999).

The message length must be smaller than or equal to the number of pixels in the image. However embedding a message the size of the image increases the likelihood of making detectable changes inconsistent with the dithering algorithm. On average the image is modified less than when using EzStego. The difference between the original stego-image and the carrier image is measured as the Euclidean distance between two vectors or matrices. It was found that the distance between the original and the stego-images is greater than four times smaller using Fridrichs method. This measurement was carried out for messages of increasing length. The only artefacts that may be introduced which have resulted from embedding large messages are local inconsistencies with error diffusion algorithms (Fridrich, 1999).

Fridrich claims that this method of pseudo randomly changing the LSB of a pointer by locating the closest pixel colour in the palette rather than adjusting the palette as with Ezstego produces approximately four times less distortion to the carrier image (Fridrich, 1999).

Further work by Fridrich has been carried out to more carefully select of pixels for embedding data. One method would be to assign weights to pixels according to how easily they can be modified. Pixels which have close colours would be chosen above colours which are isolated in the colour space. Another method would be to avoid changing pixels in areas which have uniform colour (Fridrich and Du, 2000).

2.3 S-Tools

The S-Tools package was written by Andy Brown (Wayner, 2002). Version 3 of this system can use cover images in either GIF or BMP format (ST-BMP.EXE), in sound stored as WAV files (ST-WAV.EXE) or in unallocated areas of a disc (ST-FDD.EXE) (Johnson et al, 2001). Version 4 can process image or sound files using a single program (S-TOOLS.EXE). S-Tools runs under Windows 3.1 (Wayner, 2002), (Brown, 1994). It has extensive help files and is shareware (Wayner, 2002).

S-Tools has three programs which can encrypt any information being stored in a file using a range of encryption algorithms (Wayner, 2002). The encryption programs include IDEA, DES, triple DES, MPJ (Johnson et al, 2001) and NSEA (Wayner, 2002). S-Tools displays the maximum size message it can hold in an open cover file in its toolbar (Johnson et al, 2001). After a message has been hidden the new stego-image is displayed and the user can toggle between the original and stegoed images (Johnson et al, 2001). One of the methods for S-Tools involves changing the least significant bit of each of the three colours in a pixel in a 24-bit image (Wayner, 2002) for example a 24-bit BMP file (Johnson et al, 2001). The problem with 24-bit images is that they are not commonly used on the web and tend to stand out (Wayner, 2002), a feature not helpful to steganography. 8-bit images such as GIF files are often used. They can be promoted to 24-bit images (Johnson et al, 2001). But colour reduction can also be applied.

The software for S-Tools can reduce the number of colours in the image to 256 (Wayner, 2002). The software uses the algorithm developed by Heckbert (Heckbert, 1982) to reduce the number of colours in an image in a way that will not visually disrupt the image (Wayner, 2002). The algorithm plots all the colours in three dimensions (RGB) (Wayner, 2002). It searches for a collection of n boxes, which contains all of the colours in one of the boxes (Wayner, 2002). The process starts with the complete 256 x 256 x 256 space as one box. The boxes are then recursively subdivided by splitting them in the best possible way (Wayner, 2002). Splitting continues until there are n boxes representing the space. When it is finished the programme chooses one colour to represent all the colours in each box. The colour may be chosen in different ways: the centre of the box, the average box colour or the average of the pixels in the box.

The subdivision algorithm used by this steganography method can use two different ways to divide the boxes. By one method the largest dimension is chosen by measuring the greatest difference in RGB values (Wayner, 2002). The other method compares the luminosity of the different choices (Wayner, 2002). When the colours are chosen S-Tools uses a process called dithering to replace the old colours with the new colours (Wayner, 2002). After the data has been mixed into the LSBs, the numbers of colours are lowered until it ends up with fewer than 256 colours. This process must be repeated several times until the right number is found.

An 8-bit image can be reduced to 32 colours (Johnson et al, 2001). This allows 3 bits of each pixel to be available to hide information. S-tools cannot predict the number of final colours in advance because it constantly tries to add 3 bits to each pixel (Wayner, 2002). It takes the red, green and blue values for each pixel and changes the LSB of each one independently. One colour could become 8 colours (Wayner, 2002). This is quite possible if a colour is common to the image (Wayner, 2002).

The new colours produced are entered into new palette spaces. When the palette is ordered by luminance blocks of very similar colours which appear the same have differences of 1 bit (Johnson and Jajodia, 1998). When S-tools is used on greyscale images the embedded image is no longer in greyscale because the RGB vales may vary by one bit (Johnson and Jajodia, 1998).

2.4 StegoDos

StegoDos may also be known as Black Wolfs Picture encoder version 0.90a (Anon, 1993). It is made up of a series of DOS programmes. It can be used with 320 x 200 images with 256 colours only (Johnson et al, 2001). The LSBs are modified and an end of file (EOF) character is added to the end of a message (Johnson et al, 2001). Johnson found this a method which requires considerable effort to use with less than optimal results (Johnson et al, 2001).

2.5 White Noise Storm

White Noise Storm is a set of DOS software (Johnson et al, 2001) with an encryption method which adds the bits randomly to the image (Johnson et al, 2001). Steganography is carried out on PCX files (Cole, 1997) and the LSBs are removed from the image and stored in a file. The message is encrypted and applied to the stored bits producing a new set of LSBs. The modified bits are added to the cover image to create the stego-image (Johnson et al, 2001). This software is based on spread spectrum technology and frequency hopping (somewhat like DES block encryption)(Cox et al, 1996).

2.6 Gifshuffle

This program uses the order of the palette to hide messages. The order of the colours in the palette does not affect the way the image is displayed. Images with a different colour map or palette order are visibly identical. The message is firstly compressed using Huffman encoding. This is used because Gifshuffle provides limited storage space in some cases. Gifshuffle has an encryption algorithm built in called ICE (Kwan, 1998).

In a palette there exists a certain number of possible orderings or arrangements of 256 colours. Up to

$\log_2(256!) = 210$ bytes (or more exactly 1676 bits) can be hidden in the palette by permuting its entries (Fridrich and Du, 1999). Each of these orders of the palette corresponds to a certain sequence of bits. An order for the message is chosen corresponding to the sequence of bits that make up the message. When the message is chosen and optionally compressed and / or encrypted a sequence of 1's and 0's is produced (Kwan, 1998). 1 is perpended to this sequence (Kwan, 1998). This sequence of bits produces a number m and this number is used to calculate the order of the palette used for that particular message.

The colours in the palette are then counted giving a value n (Kwan, 1998). If $m > n! -1$ the message is too large and the procedure aborted. The colours in the palette are then sorted into their natural order. Each RGB colour is assigned a value (red x 65536 + green x 256 + blue) and the colours are sorted according to these values. Duplicate colours are stored at the top of the palette and are not used for storing the hidden message (Kwan, 1998). The program iterates i through the values 1 to n. Each colour n - i in the palette is allocated a new position. The positions are numbered as in an array from 0 to n - 1. The position is calculated using m mod i. m is then divided by i which produces a value m to be used in the second iteration and so on. Each colour (n-1)...0 is in turn inserted into the new palette order. Colours previously occupying the target position and above are moved up one place. The GIF image is uncompressed, the colour indices remapped to the new palette and the image is recompressed. Extracting the message follows the same procedure but in reverse order.

Using this method of steganography the appearance of the image is not changed. The security is a problem because the order of the palette may be changed by image processing software and ordered by luminance, frequency or occurrence or some other scalar factor (Fridrich and Du, 1999). The order may change during displaying and saving the image and data may be lost (Fridrich and Du, 1999). Also a randomly ordered palette might look suspicious.

2.6.1 Mandelsteg

This method uses fractal images for cover images (Murray and van Ryper, 1996). Mandelsteg creates Mandelbrot fractal images or graphics. If a file name is passed as a parameter the file is hidden in the Mandelbrot image (Johnson et al, 2001). Depending on the parameters the image may vary in size and colour (Johnson et al, 2001). Mandelsteg does not manipulate any cover images other than the fractal images it creates (Johnson et al, 2001). This makes it unique as a method. Information is hidden in the LSB of an image of the Mandelbrot set. The LSB of the Mandelbrot set can be flipped (Wayner, 2002). A synthetic image is produced which is computed to seven bits of accuracy and a message is then hidden in the eight bit (Wayner, 2002). All Mandelsteg images have 256 palette entries in the colour index. The image palette contains 128 unique colours with 2 entries for each colour. Therefore looking at a palette points to the fact that fractal images have been produced by Mandelsteg (Johnson et al, 2001).

A fractal property is a similar repeating pattern. Fractals are made up of smaller versions of themselves (Beck, 2000). Fractal is derived from the Latin word frangere which means to break or fragment. A fractal is any pattern that shows greater complexity as it is enlarged (Fractal). Fractals are created from a positive feed back loop. They are created using iterated function systems (Beck, 2000). Data goes in one end is modified and comes out the other. This output is fed back into the system as input over and over again (Fractal). The Mandelbrot set looks random but has structure (Wayner, 2002). Each pixel represents the number of iterations before a simple equation converges ($f(z) = z^2 + C$). A Julia set uses one function that does not change. Each point in the Julia set is passed through the function many times to see if the point will eventually go to infinity. The function determines the image generated. The Mandelbrot sets equation changes with the point being plotted (Beck, 2000).

A Mandelbrot set looks random but actually has plenty of structure. The problem with fractal images is that they are synthetically, mathematically created and therefore maths can be used to analyse them. However this may be alleviated somewhat by the fact that they can be very complex (Wayner, 2002). The data recovery program GifExtract could be run to remove the bits. There are several different settings but it is likely one will eventually work (Wayner, 2002). To prevent this Wayner (Wayner, 2002) recommends running Stealth to strip away the framing text from the PGP message. Another weakness is that the Mandelbrot image acts as a one-time pad for the data. If a pattern can be found in the key data the data could be extracted. The most significant bits could be examined and the location from which the image came determined. The LSBs could be recalculated and the message extracted (Wayner, 2002).

2.7   Steganos

This method hides the data in each third byte (Johnson et al, 2001). BMP images are used which have a terminating zero byte at the end of each row of the raster data (Johnson et al, 2001). Because of this byte the manipulated colour channel keeps changing when the zero byte is reached. Figure 11 below illustrates the effect of the hidden data in every third LSB in 24-bit and 8-bit images. The images have been enlarged about 800 times. The image shows the alternating bands in the three RGB colour channels of the image. Figure 12 shows the effect of hidden data in every third LSB in the blue bytes of an 8-bit image.

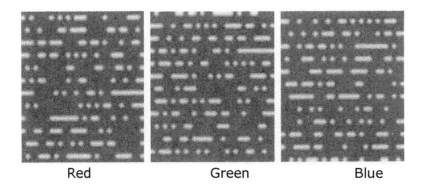

Red   Green   Blue

Figure 11: Illustration of Steganos Hiding Data in Every Third Least Significant Bit (24-bit) (Johnson et al, 2001)

Figure 12: Illustration of Steganos Hiding Data in Every Third Least Significant Bit (8-bit) (Johnson et al, 2001)

3 Steganalysis

There are two stages involved in breaking a steganographic system: detecting that steganography has been used and reading the embedded message (Zollner et al, 1998). Steganalysis methods should be used by the steganographer in order to determine whether a message is secure and consequently whether a steganographic process has been successful. The goal of a stegoanalyst is to detect stego-messages, read the embedded message and prove that the message has been embedded to third parties (Pfitzmann, 1996). Detection involves observing relationships between combinations of cover, message, stego-media and steganography tools (Johnson et al, 2001). This can be achieved by passive observation. Active interference by the stegoanalyst involves removing the message without changing the stego-image too much (the stegoanalyst might want to conceal his existence), or removing the message without consideration to the stego-image appearance or structure (Pfitzmann, 1996). Whether a message has been hidden in an image or not the image could be manipulated to destroy a possible hidden message (Johnson and Jajodia, 1998).

There are two necessary conditions to be fulfilled for a secure steganographic process. The key must remain unknown to the attacker and the attacker should not be familiar with the cover image (Zollner et al, 1998). If the cover image is known, the message could then be embedded in a random way so that it is secure however it is preferable that the image is unknown. Attacks on steganography can involve detection and/or destruction of the embedded message. A *stego-only attack* is when only the stego-image is available to be analysed (Johnson and Jajodia, 1998). A *known cover attack* is when the original cover image is also available. It involves comparing the original cover image with the stego-image. As explained above hiding information results in alterations to the properties of a carrier which may result in some sort of degradation to the carrier (Johnson and Jajodia, 1998). Original images and stego-images can be analysed by looking at colour composition, luminance and pixel relationships and unusual characteristics can be detected. If a hidden message is revealed at some later date the attacker could analyse the stego-image for future attacks. This is called *known message attack*. The *chosen stego attack* is used when the steganography algorithm and the image are known. A *chosen message attack* is when the stegoanalyst generates stego-images using a given steganography algorithm using a known message (Johnson and Jajodia, 1998). The purpose is to examine the patterns produced in the stego-images that may point to the use of certain steganography algorithms.

Most steganographic algorithms embed messages by replacing carefully selected pixels bits with message bits (Westfield and Pfitzmann, 1999). Any changes to the data associated with the image through embedding will change the properties of the image in some way. This process may create patterns or unusual exaggerated noise (Johnson and Jajodia, 1998). An image with plenty of bad effects is a problem that can be detected with the human eye. The patterns visible to the human eye could broadcast the existence of a message and point to signatures of certain methods or tools used (Johnson and Jajodia, 1998). Human sight is trained to recognise known things. This process of analysis depends on the ability of humans to discern between normal noise and visual corruption and patterns created by steganography (Westfield and Pfitzmann, 1999). It can be difficult to distinguish randomness and image contents and to distinguish LSBs and random bits by machine.

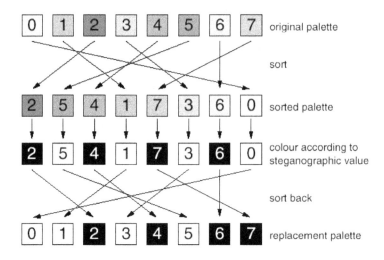

Figure 13: Assignment function of replacement colours; colours that have an even index in the sorted palette become black, the rest becomes white (Westfield and Pfitzmann, 1999)

Visual attacks can involve removing the parts of the image containing the message i.e. the least significant bit of each pixel (Westfield and Pfitzmann, 1999). Sometimes the least significant bits are not very random. The human eye may then distinguish whether there is a message distorting the image content. The filtering process which can be used for this purpose involves extraction of the potential message bits based on a presumed steganographic method and then illustrating the bits on the position of their source pixels (Westfield and Pfitzmann, 1999).

An embedding filter presents the values pixels yield when the extraction function is applied to them. For example the embedding filter for EzStego replaces the original palette by a black and white palette. The original palette is sorted by frequency. The palette is then sorted by luminance. Every even position in the palette (0, 2, 4, 6, ...) is set to black and every uneven position in the palette is set to white. (Westfield and Pfitzmann, 1999).

The replacement palette is now reordered into its original order. This is shown in Figure 13 above.

If numerous comparisons can be made between the cover images and the stego-images patterns can begin to emerge (Johnson et al, 2001). At a later stage if the cover is not available the known signature will be sufficient to indicate a message and the tool used to embed it (Johnson et al, 2001). Some of the methods of carrying out steganography produce characteristics that act as signatures for that steganography method (Johnson and Jajodia, 1998).

The image may not give away the existence of stenography but the palette could. Therefore steganography can be detected by examining the palette itself. In colour palettes the colours are ordered from most used to least used. The changes between colour values rarely change in one-bit increments in an unstegoed image. But this feature would be created by embedding in the LSBs during steganography. Greyscale palettes do change in one bit increments but all the RGB values are the same. In monochromatic images usually two of the RGB values are the same and the third usually has a much stronger saturation of colour. Therefore there are expected patterns in palettes which if adjusted could indicate the use of steganography.

If an original image contains 200 colours steganography could result in the formation of 400 colours which would be too many to store in the palette. When the image is saved as an 8-bit image it will produce a new palette with 256 colours and information hidden could be lost. This is prevented by reducing the colours initially so that space is available for new colours to be created. Adjacent colours are added which are very close to the original. A stego-image is produced which is very close to the original cover image (Brown, 1994). Reducing the colours in the palette and creating new colours resulting from changing the LSBs of existing colours will results in blocks of similar colours differing by one bit in the palette. This is shown in Figure 14. The palette on the right has blocks of similar colours produced by the creation of new colours by adjustment of the LSBs. A unique pattern has been created in the palette.

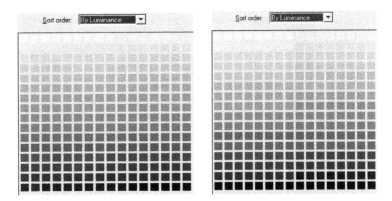

Figure 14: Cover (left) and Stego-Image Palette (right) after S-Tools (Johnson and Jajodia, 1998)

Using a steganography method where pointers to the palette are changed may increase noise because adjacent colours in the image become very different after the message has been embedded (Johnson and Jajodia, 1998). This is alleviated by the use of greyscale images (Johnson and Jajodia, 1998). A method of detection might be to look at areas in the image where colour does not flow well from one area to another. If pixels beside each other have very different colours this could indicate the existence of steganography (Wayner, 2002). If images are created which have very different adjacent palette entries (Cha et al, 1995) small shifts in the LSBs of the pixel colours will cause radical colour changes in the image advertising the existence of a hidden message. The palette may not be altered but changes to the pixel colours may show dramatic changes to the image (Johnson and Jajodia, 1998).

 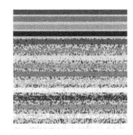

Figure 15: Original 8-bit Cover Image (left), and the 8-bit Stego-Image (right) Created with Hide and Seek. (Johnson and Jajodia, 1998)

Steganography tools that modify the lower bits of 8-bit images can produce noisy distorted stego-images (Hansmann, 1996)(Machado, 1996) (Maroney). In Figure 15 below the left image is the original and the right image shows the impact of embedding using Hide and Seek which is a steganographic method that results in changes to the LSBs.

An 8-bit image could be converted to a 24-bit image to produce a less noisy or distorted stego-image. Colour values can be directly manipulated and any changes will most likely be visually undetectable. However the image could end up quite big and unsuitable for electronic transmission (Johnson and Jajodia, 1998). Detection of a hidden message may be related to the size of the image and the format and content of the carrier image. If the message is larger an image will receive more modification. There is then a higher probability that the modifications will be detected (Fridrich and Du, 1999) and consequently there is then an increased probability the message will be detected (Fridrich, 1999).

Statistical attacks can be carried out using automated methods. A stego-image should have the same statistical characteristics as the carrier so that the use of a stenographic algorithm can't be detected (Westfield and Pfitzmann, 1999). Therefore a potential message can be read from both the stego-image and the carrier and the message should not be statistically different from a potential message read from a carrier (Westfield and Pfitzmann, 1999). If it were statistically different the steganographic system would be insecure. Automation can be used to investigate pixel neighbourhoods and determining if an outstanding pixel is common to the image, follows some sort of pattern or resembles noise. A knowledge base of predictable patterns can be compiled and this can assist in automating the detection process (Johnson and Jajodia, 1998). Steganalysis tools can determine the existence of hidden messages and even the tools used to embed them (Sanders, 1997). A person wishing to detect someone else's stegoed images may analyse the type of equipment being used to create the image such as a scanner or digital camera (Fridrich, 1999). A set of statistical measures could be determined which satisfy all of the images produced by this piece of equipment and consequently statistical fingerprints could be determined caused by the presence of a hidden message (Fridrich, 1999).

In order to prevent detection steganographic and cryptographic keys can be used. A steganographic key controls embedding and extracting of the message. The key could scatter the message randomly over the carrier. A cryptographic key is used to encrypt a message before embedding. Therefore even when the message is detected it can't be read.

In the case of bitwise methods destruction of the embedded message is fairly easy because the LSBs of the images can be changed with compression. The image may be converted to lossy compression format such as JPEG. JPEG images which have been processed with Jpeg-Jsteg can be recompressed and this will destroy the message embedded in the DCT coefficients because they will be recalculated (Johnson and Jajodia, 1998).

A series of tests were carried out by Johnson to distort embedded data. The purpose was to evaluate the robustness of bit-wise and transform tools (Johnson and Jajodia, 1998). The object of the tests was to show what the techniques will withstand and what are some common vulnerabilities. Images tested included digital photographs (24-bit or 8-bit greyscale JPEG and 24-bit BMP), clip art (8-bit GIF) and digital art (24-bit BMP or JPEG, 8-bit BMP or GIF). To determine robustness images were manipulated following embedding with a number of image processing techniques: converting between lossless and lossy formats, converting between bit densities, blurring, smoothing, adding noise, removing noise, sharpening, edge enhancement, masking, rotating, scaling, re-sampling, warping, converting from digital to analog and back (printing and scanning), mirroring, flipping, adding bitwise messages, adding transform messages and applying the unZign and StirMark tools to test the robustness of watermarking software. Tests were also carried out to determine the smallest size of image that can be used. The tests were used to alter the information to such a point that it could not be retrieved again. The message was then checked.

Conversion to compressed JPEG images or minor processing disables the bit wise tools. Tools that relied on bit wise methods to hide the data could not recover any of the messages. The transform tools did survive several of the image processing tests but failed when combinations of image processes were carried out on them. These tests showed that the transform methods are in fact more robust.

4   Watermarking

Watermarking is the process of hiding information in a carrier in order to protect the ownership of text, music, films and art (Wayner, 2002). In other words watermarking can be used to hide or embed visible or hidden copyright information (Wayner, 2002), (Johnson et al, 2001). Steganography techniques can be used for the purposes of watermarking. Often information is hidden about the carrier itself providing further information about the carrier which is not explicitly displayed. (Johnson et al, 2001).

Watermarks in images are hidden mainly so that they don't get in the way of an image rather than to avoid detection. Watermarks are generally hidden in the more significant areas of the image and therefore are generally not lost by compression (Johnson et al, 2001). Most consumers and pirates will know that there is a watermark if they try to make a copy of the image. The main object of watermarking is to prevent copies of the image being made using copyrighting and prevent the watermark being removed. The ID of an author can be hidden in an image. If the image is circulated the ID of the original owner will still be in it. Ideally a watermark should stay with a document even after it is cropped or compressed or edited. In some cases watermarks are clearly visible. In this case they are not a type of steganography but are part of the image itself (Johnson et al, 2001).

The watermark might be located in some significant area of the image or repeated over the whole surface of the image. Repeating the watermark all over the image resists cropping (Wayner, 2002). Masking techniques can be used to hide information and produce a stronger watermark. In one example by Johnson the luminance of the area containing the watermark is increased by 5% (Johnson et al, 2001). This results in the watermark being undetectable to the human eye.

The human eye can be drawn to areas of high frequency in an image that is areas such as edges and lines (Grhul and Bender, 1998), (Johnson et al, 1999). Applying a gradual or blurred mask permits a greater increase in luminance before the watermark becomes visible as distortion in the image. The watermark produced by this technique will be more resistant to changes in lower bits. Increasing the luminance in a sharp mask will cause the watermark to become visible in busy high frequency areas of the image on a high resolution monitor with much less of an increase in luminance than if a blurred mask were used. In low frequency areas of an image the watermark will become visible with much less of an increase in luminance (Johnson et al, 2001).

Adaptive embedding can be used where information is hidden along edges or in areas of higher frequency. Masking techniques involve embedding information in more significant areas of an image. These areas tend to be along edges of regions of more structure. This makes it robust to compression and some image processing (Johnson et al, 2001).

Rather than adding bits to an image some watermarking techniques add distortions. The shape and location of the distortion will show who owns the document. Some watermarks require providing extra data to the detector. This could be a key or the original un-watermarked image. This prevents unauthorized people from adding a watermark or creating fake documentation. Keys may allow only certain people to access the watermark (Wayner, 2002). A watermark may carry multiple messages from multiple different people who can insert and retrieve data without any coordination between them (Wayner, 2002). Some methods can carry multiple messages especially if there is error correction in the system to prevent collisions between messages. Another method of watermarking is to use transform techniques by hiding information in the frequency domain (Wayner, 2002). Figure 16 below shows a watermarked image.

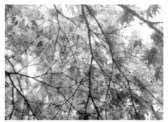

a. Original Image   b. Watermarked Image

c. Difference Between a. and b. the Watermark

Figure 16: **Image Watermarking (Johnson, 1999 a)**

Attacks on watermarks will involve trying to remove or distort the watermark. They may involve replacing the watermark with another piece of information. The hidden information should be made such an integral part of an image that to interfere with the information would destroy the image (Johnson et al, 2001). If the watermark is hidden in the LSB then all a cracker has to do is flip one LSB and the information cannot be recovered. Various image processing techniques may be used to attack a watermark. Storing new information in the carrier is another way of attacking the watermark. It is particularly successful when using the same algorithm as was originally used to produce the existing watermark (Wayner, 2002). It must be ensured that watermarks are not removed by compression algorithms. One of the problems which can occur is someone registering an unwatermarked image as their own even if it was created by some one else (Johnson et al, 2001). Another problem with watermarking is that their existence is often advertised so that potential users know that the image has a watermark and has copyright information built in if they decide to add it to their own document (Johnson et al, 2001). Sometimes easy to break watermarks have their own use in that they can determine if anyone has tampered with the image. This gives an assurance that the image has not been altered.

One particular watermarking method proposed by (Wayner, 2002) is carried out as follows. Decompose the image into certain important components. One way of doing this is to model the signal using DCT as the sum of a collection of cosine functions multiplied by a set of coefficients. The coefficients measure the size of the components which the document has been decomposed into i.e. the collection of cosine functions. The model will ensure that large coefficients have a large effect on the document a small coefficients a lesser effect. Small coefficients will be changed by changes in the document and are not as important (Wayner, 2002). Quantize the coefficients. This is done by finding the closest replacement from a small set of values (Wayner, 2002). The watermark is inserted by tweaking each coefficient. Reverse transform is use to reconstruct the original document. Some methods include error correction bits into the watermark bits. This method is quite resistant to cropping as many of the same coefficients will emerge even after the image has been cropped (Wayner, 2002).

Detecting ownership of images on the web is a difficult task. Software must be able to determine if an image is belong to a particular author even if it has undergone some modification. The image needs to be detected as a variant of the original one. Techniques used to recognise and retrieve images are based on colour, image content, spatial relationships, and annotation of image objects (Flickner et al, 1995), (Frankel and Swain, 1996), (Niblack et al, 1993). These methods will retrieve very similar but not exact images (Johnson et al, 2001). The system must be able to identify an image even if it has been slightly changed (Johnson et al, 2001). Digital watermarking techniques for recognition of images over the network fall short of tracking down the distorted image and matching it to the original (Johnson et al, 2001).

Fingerprinting images is a method of identifying invariant features in an image. These can be parts of the image itself or added features. The salient characteristics of the image used for identifying it are known as the fingerprint (Johnson et al, 2001). A salient feature is an object native to the image that does not vary with changes in colour, format, compression and transformations. These features might be edges and corners with high gradient magnitude. Recognition consists of two stages. A set of feature points is selected from the image at multiple resolutions and then matches are found between the fingerprint of the original and of images in a set of unknown images. The techniques for fingerprinting could be used to choose locations in an image in which to embed information for steganography or locations to embed stronger watermarks.

5 Cryptography

This is a study of steganographic methods where the emphasis is on preventing others from knowing that a message exists by hiding its existence. The accepted rational for encryption is very different, its objective is not to hide a messages existence but to make the contents of the message unreadable. Thus on the face of it there appears to be no immediate relationship between the two technologies.

However it is important to mention cryptography also as it is commonly used along with steganography to generate an encrypted message to be hidden in the carrier. This helps to make the message secure in the event of its being discovered. However the act of encrypting a message also makes it harder to recognise its original form.

A by product of this is that it enhances steganography because many of the accepted methods of attacking steganographic messages is to look for patterns in the medium the message is hidden in. If the underlying pattern in the message to be hidden is modified prior to hiding it in the chosen medium then it should be harder to attack the steganographic method using pattern searches.

What follows is a general explanation of cryptography including a description of some of the most common methods.

5.1 An Overview of Cryptography

Encryption is "The process of disguising a message in such a way as to hide its substance" (Schneier, 1996). It is "concerned with the design of any system that needs to withstand malicious attempts to abuse it" (Goldreich, 2001). The cryptographic operation takes input data (the message) and produces a set of output data. Generally the output is larger than the input (Oakes, 2001). The message to be encrypted is known as plaintext and the encrypted message is known as ciphertext (Schneier, 1996). The ciphertext should not contain any information about the plaintext but if it does it should not be possible to efficiently extract it (Goldreich, 2001). Decryption is carried out to turn ciphertext back into plaintext (Schneier, 1996) (Goldreich, 2001). The ISO terms to encode or decode using encryption are encipher and decipher (Mel, 2001). Cryptology is the art and science of keeping messages secure (cryptography) and the art and science of breaking ciphertext also called cryptanalysis (Schneier, 1996). Cryptography is used to protect commercial and business messages as well as messages by diplomats, soldiers and spies (Smith, 1997). The challenge for successful cryptography is providing a secure communication over an insecure medium (Goldreich, 2001).

The plaintext P or message M can be a stream of bits, a text file, a bitmap, a stream of digitised voice or a digital image. In the case of computing, plaintext is anything that can be converted into binary data. Ciphertext denoted by C is sometimes the same size and sometimes larger than the plaintext (Schneier, 1996). The encryption function E (a computationally difficult one way function (Goldreich, 2001)) operates on M to produce C (Schneier, 1996). This is shown as: $E(M) = C$. For decryption the decryption function D operates on C to produce M: $D(C) = M$

The mathematical function used to carry out encryption or decryption is called the cryptographic algorithm or the cipher (Schneier, 1996). The algorithm generally refers to particular implementations of the cryptographic operation

(Oakes, 2001). Cryptographic algorithms are generally distributed and used as software packages but can also be hard-coded into digital circuits (Smith, 1997). A restricted algorithm is one whose security is based on keeping the way the algorithm works a secret. This type of algorithm cannot be used by a large or changing group of people. This is because if someone left the group the algorithm would have to be changed. Obviously also if the algorithm was revealed it would have to be changed. A group cannot buy this type of algorithm off the shelf as an eavesdropper could buy the same one. Therefore with this type of algorithm every group of users must have their own unique algorithm (Schneier, 1996).

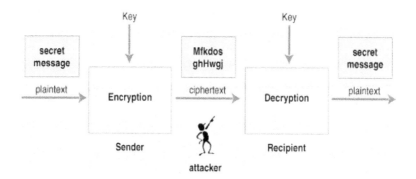

Modern cryptography solves the need to keep the algorithm secret by using what is called a key (K). A key is a long string of numbers with certain mathematical properties (Oakes, 2001). The range of possible values which can be included in the key is called the keyspace. Both encryption and decryption algorithms use this key (Schneier, 1996). A pseudo random number generator can be used to expand short keys into much larger keys (Goldreich, 2001). If the key is increased by one bit this can double the number of possible keys (Mel, 2001). The functions now become: $E_K(M) = C$ and $D_K(C) = M$. Many different ciphertexts can be produced from one plaintext depending on the algorithm and/or key being used (Ritter, 2002).

Some algorithms have different encryption and decryption keys. The security of the algorithm is based entirely on the key not on the algorithm itself which means that the algorithm can be published, tested and analysed by anyone. Products which are made using this algorithm can therefore be mass produced.

A cryptosystem is the algorithm plus any possible plaintexts, ciphertexts and keys. A good algorithm produces ciphertext that gives away as little as possible about the key or plaintext that produced it (Smith, 1997).

5.2   Symmetric and Assymmetric Algorithms

There are two types of algorithms which are based on a key. These are called symmetric and public key (assymmetric) algorithms (Schneier, 1996). Symmetric or conventional algorithms (also called secret key, single key, or one key) have an encryption key which can be calculated from the decryption key and vice versa. The encryption key and decryption key are usually the same (Schneier, 1996) (Oakes, 2001). The range of key sizes are typically between 40 and 128 bits (Smith, 1997). The sender and receiver decide on a key before any secure communication can be made (Schneier, 1996) (Oakes, 2001)(Goldreich, 2001). The security of this algorithm depends entirely on keeping that key secret (Oakes, 2001) (Schneier, 1996). If the key becomes known anyone can encrypt and decrypt messages with this algorithm.

Public key or asymmetric algorithms have one key used for encryption and a different key for decryption (Schneier, 1996) (Oakes, 2001). The encryption key should not be able to be determined from the decryption key (in any reasonable amount of time) (Schneier, 1996). The public key can be used by one party and the private key by the other party (Oakes, 2001). If a sender wants to send a message he can use the public key and the receiver can use a private key. Therefore unlike the previous secret key method where both the sender and receiver had to ensure that each had the same key, in this case the key needs only be known by the receiver (Oakes, 2001). This makes the system more secure as the key does not have to be distributed to another user. Therefore the encryption key can be made public hence the name public key. Anyone can encrypt a message but only the receiver with the correct decryption key can decrypt it. In a system like this the encryption key is called the public key and the decryption key is the private key or secret key. Messages can also be encrypted with the private key and decrypted with the public key. This method is used for digital signatures (Schneier, 1996).

The digital signature can be used for example by the personnel department of a company to change payroll details or on an online subscription service (Oakes, 2001).

5.3   Stream and Block Ciphers

Stream algorithms or stream ciphers operate on plaintext a single bit or byte at a time (Schneier, 1996). A Vernam cipher is a stream cipher. This cipher uses a key stored on a long loop of paper tape (Smith, 1997). Block algorithms or ciphers operate on plaintext in groups of bits. The block on which this algorithm operates is typically 64 bits in length which is large enough to preclude analysis but still small enough to be usable (Schneier, 1996). DES is a block cipher (Smith, 1997).

5.4   Substitution and Transposition

In substitution algorithms a character in the plaintext is substituted for another character to produce the ciphertext. This process is reversed in decryption. For example, instead of substituting one character for another character, characters can also be encrypted together in pairs or larger groups increasing the number of possibilities from 26 for the letters of the English alphabet to 676 in the case of pairs (Ritter, 2002). In a transposition cipher the order of the characters is changed. The letters used for the plaintext and ciphertext are the same therefore frequency of the characters can be used by the cryptanalyst to break the algorithm. The ciphertext can be put through a second transposition cipher (Schneier, 1996) to make it more secure. A computer can break almost all of these ciphers. Transposition is less common than substitution because it can take up a lot of memory and messages have a restricted length (Schneier, 1996). This is because the process itself depends on the length of the message. Using substitution the message length does not matter (Mel, 2001).

5.5   One-Time Pads

A one-time pad is a large non-repeating set of random key letters written on pieces of paper and attached together in a pad (Kahn, 1967). The sender uses each letter on the pad to encrypt one character. Encryption is the addition of the plaintext character and the key character modulo 26 (Schneier, 1996). Each key letter is used once for one message. When the message has been encrypted the pages of the pad that were used are destroyed. The receiver uses an identical pad for decryption and also destroys the pages used. The key letters must be generated randomly (Smith, 1997) and the pages used must never be used again. If these rules are followed this method of encryption is perfectly secure (Schneier, 1996). Therefore it is used for ultra secure transmissions. A pad containing bits can be used instead of a pad of letters. The binary data of the plaintext and the key can be XOR'ed (Schneier, 1996).

5.6   Cryptanalysis

The strength of modern cryptography lies in the large body of mathematical work on which the algorithms are based and on the fact that some computations (functions) are more difficult to reverse than they were to perform initially (Smith, 1997). Cryptanalysis is the science of recovering a message without knowing the key (Schneier, 1996). When this is carried out it is known as an attack. Cryptanalysis may involve recovering the plaintext or the key or finding weaknesses in the cryptographic system (Schneier, 1996). As well as helping an attacker to break the algorithm, cryptanalysis also helps to strengthen the algorithms themselves (Smith, 1997). Designers and users know that a systems weaknesses must be understood before its strengths can be relied upon (Smith, 1997). An algorithm should be designed to resist cryptanalysis (Schneier, 1996). There are certain properties a good algorithm should have. Generally the algorithm should rely on the secrecy of the key (Kahn, 1967) rather than the secrecy of the algorithm. Keeping the algorithm secret will prevent it from being analysed but will also prevent analysts finding weaknesses in it (Smith, 1997). If an algorithm is available for analysis it should be analysed by a range of experts to ensure its strength (Smith, 1997). The analysis should find no serious weaknesses (Smith, 1997). In many cases algorithms become known to the public and are constantly analysed. Even when new methods are created it can be presumed that they too will be analysed and potentially cracked particularly with the availability of faster computers. Some of the best algorithms are the ones that have been made public, have been attacked by cryptanalysts for years and are still unbroken (Schneier, 1996). Generally the effectiveness of cryptosystems wanes over time so that users must constantly look out for newer and stronger techniques (Smith, 1997).

Breaking an algorithm can involve different things such as finding the key, finding an alternative algorithm, discovering the plaintext from the cipher text, or gaining some information about the key or the plaintext. Given an infinite number of resources only a one-time pad is unbreakable. Cryptography is most interested with cryptosystems that are computationally unfeasible to break (Schneier, 1996).

Different algorithms have different degrees of security depending on how hard they are to break. It may be possible to extract information with a lot of effort but it may not be feasible (Goldreich, 2001). The work factor is an estimate of how hard the attacker must work to get past the cipher and achieve a valuable goal (Smith, 1997). Stronger systems have a larger work factor (Smith, 1997). The work factor should be "large enough to make the costs of an attack greater than the potential benefits to the attacker" (Smith, 1997).

5.7 Steganography and Cryptography

The usefulness of cryptography from a steganographic point of view lies less in its direct information security role than in its indirect role as an aid to steganography by jumbling up the message before it is hidden in the carrier. Thus, from a purely steganographic point of view, a cryptographic method is being sought which jumbles up the message and thus makes it more difficult to find using steganalysis rather than a particularly secure cryptographic algorithm. Of course in a real world situation a full and secure cryptographic method would be used for this purpose but for the purposes of this work it should, given the time constraints placed on the work, be adequate to use a simpler cryptographic method such as Knapsack rather than a method such as IDEA or DES whose full implementation would be a significant and not necessarily productive distraction which would not add to this study of steganography.

6 Steganography Methodologies

Having carried out a review of steganographic and cryptographic methods it has been found that one of the main methods typically used for steganography involves the process of hiding a message in image pixels. Images are the most widespread carrier medium used. There are various ways of doing this. In some methods the purpose is to minimize changes to the image and in some the purpose is to store the message in a random way so as to make it more difficult to detect. In some methods more information can be stored by using more than one bit of the colours representing the pixels. This allows more information to be stored but also results in the formation of more new colours and the need to use an image which is comprised of less colours to start with. In some methods the process of storing information can result in the production of new colours in the image and in some methods the existing colours only are used. Some methods involve the use of a key. These different characteristics may be used individually or combined to produce similar systems to many of those currently being used.

While steganography can be carried out on any digital media it is reasonable for the purposes of cross comparing methods to implement these methods on a common media type. The chosen media for this system are GIF images. GIF images have been chosen because as they are widely used in web pages, are recognised by all browsers and they are easily distributable which ensures that they lend themselves to this type of activity without drawing attention to themselves. Audio and video carriers require more intensive processing to hide data in them as the files the carrier is stored in tend to be larger. BMP files have a very large number of colours which has advantages from a steganography point of view but their corresponding size makes them unsuitable for distribution across a web type medium. It has also been found that the compression / decompression algorithm causes problems for steganography. GIF undergoes lossless compression. The advantage of lossless compression is that the original digital image is reproduced exactly and therefore the original arrangement of bits making up the image is maintained. The LZW technique must normally be paid for however the software is included in Java so that working on GIF programs in Java does not require any payment. Images saved in JPEG use lossy compression in which the image is not reconstructed in exactly the same way as the original. Space is saved in storing the image however some of the bits and hence some of the data can be lost. JPEG files are sensitive to small changes in the image data which results in less capacity for holding a message[9]. It raises less suspicion than for example a BMP format[11]. Many steganograhy packages use GIF images including Hide and Seek, S-Tools, GifShuffle, EzStggo, and the method developed by Fridrich. A GIF image has a restricted number of colours. The maximum number it can have is 256. GIF is a bitmap image. Bitmap is a system in which an image is described as a bit pattern or series of numbers that gives the shade or colour of each pixel. Greyscale GIF images, have pixel values from 0 to 255 which represent the intensity of the colour and do not refer to a palette[2].

Therefore the purpose of this study is to develop a package which will carry out steganography by hiding a text message in a GIF image carrier. As many of the methods which carry out steganography use the process of hiding the message in image pixels this system will focus on hiding the message in the least significant bits or parity bits of the colours in the pixels of an image. It is proposed to develop and evaluate the following methods explained below. The names of the methods are used to distinguish between the different steganographic processes that will be carried out.

6.1 Stego One Bit

When images are used as the carrier in steganography they are generally manipulated by changing one or more of the bits of the byte or bytes that make up the pixels of an image. The message can be stored in the LSB of one colour of the RGB value or in the parity bit of the entire RGB value. Hide and Seek uses GIF images and the lower order bit of each pixel. One of the methods for S-Tools involves changing the least significant bit of each of the three colours in a pixel in a 24-bit image. Changing the LSB will only change the integer value of the byte by one. This will not noticeable alter the visual appearance of a colour and hence the image itself. Changing a more significant bit would cause a proportionately greater change in the visual appearance of a colour. The main objective of steganography is to pass a message to a receiver without an intruder even knowing that a message is being passed which means that there should be no discernable change to the carrier. This is the first method to be tested and will involve encoding some of the basic processes required for later steganographic methods to be tested also. It will involve changing the LSB of one of the colours making up the RGB value of the pixel. This should have very little effect on the appearance of the image. This process will most likely result in the formation of new colours for the palette. Therefore the image used must have a palette size of 128 pixels or less. This will allow for a doubling of the colours in the palette (the creation of a new colour for every existing colour in the palette) which is the maximum number of colours that could be produced by this method. It may be found that if the palette is ordered by luminance that there will be pairs of very similar colours. How noticeable that is depends on the colour profile used in the image to start with. Practical methods should allow for the use of the full image size, thus the amount of data that can be hidden is proportionate to the number of pixels in the image rather than to the number of colours in the palette. The only restriction is then the size of the image. Using the image data for embedding is less restrictive on capacity compared to another method where data is stored in the palette itself. Using a 128 palette image should not result in too much distortion to the original image.

6.2 Stego Two Bits

Using this method two LSBs of one of the colours in the RGB value of the pixels will be used to store message bits in the image. This will involve using a palette with a maximum of 68 colours allowing for the production of a possible 196 new colours,i.e. two new colours for each existing colour. Less colour will be available to represent the starting image and hence it will be more degraded than the image used in the method Stego One Bit. The advantage of this method is that twice as much information can be stored here than in the previous method. This method could instead have used the LSB of two colours in the RGB value which would have resulted in the same amount of storage space. The starting image would still have to have a palette containing 68 colours.

6.3 Stego Three Bits

Using this method three LSBs of one of the colours in the RGB value of the pixels will be used to store message bits. This will involve using a palette with a maximum of only 32 colours allowing for the production of a possible 224 new colours, three new colours for every existing colour in the image. The data hiding capacity is three times the storage capacity of Stego One Bit but the image will be even more distorted than if a 128 colour palette was used.

6.4 Stego Four Bits

Using this method four LSBs of one of the colours in the RGB value of the pixels will be used to store message bits. This will involve using a palette with a maximum of only 16 colours allowing for the production of a possible 240 new colours. This is the smallest palette that could be used for an image using Jasc Paint Shop Pro. The colours are now very restricted but an area of one particular colour in the Image may have 16 variations distributed through it which could result in a certain amount of texture mitigating the effects of such a restricted palette.

6.5   Stego Colour Cycle

In order to make the detection of the hidden data more difficult it was decided to cycle through the colour values in each of the pixels in which to store the data. This also means that the same colour was not constantly being changed. For example the first data bit could be stored in the LSB of the blue value of the pixel, the second data bit in the red value and the third data bit in the green value, the alpha value will be skipped and the next colour used will be blue again. This is because changing the alpha value which is generally 255 would look too suspicious unless the image used contained different transparency levels.

6.6 StegoPRNG

A pseudo random number generator can be used to choose random pixels in which to embed the message. This will make the message bits more difficult to find and hopefully reduce the existence of patterns in the image. Most importantly it means that if a cracker removed the LSBs from one of the colours and tried to read them it would make no sense as they would not be in order. A pseudo random number generator will be created and will be used to select the pixels in which to hide the data. Data will then be hidden in the LSB of the blue value. If the message is much smaller than the capacity of the image a problem may occur whereby the information will be packed into one part of the image for example the top half.

This is solved by using a PRNG which will spread the message all over the image. Hide and Seek arranges it so that the message bits will not be beside one another but instead randomly dispersed throughout the image. Hence the noise will also be randomly distributed. A user chosen key can be inserted into a pseudo random number generator which will determine a sequence of random numbers.

These numbers will indicate the pixels in the image where the least significant bit is to be changed. This makes the system more secure because the reader of the message must know the key in order to determine in which bytes the message bits are hidden. The key must remain unknown to the attacker. If the cover image was known to the attacker, embedding the message in a random way would improve its security.

6.7   StegoFridrich

EzStego encodes in the parity bit of indices of a GIF image. Fridrichs newer method also involves manipulating existing colours in the palette. EzStego however firstly orders the palette by luminance so that similar colours are beside one another. But Fridrichs method involves pairing up all the colours in the palette so that the distance between the two colours in each of the pairs is minimized. This method searches for the closest colour to the colour of the pixel which has the correct parity for the bit to be hidden. The message is hidden in the parity bit of the RGB values of close colours. For the colour of each pixel into which a message bit is to be embedded the closest colours in the palette are searched until a palette entry is found with the desired parity bit. This technique does not change the palette in any way either by ordering it or by increasing the colours present in it.

The parity bits of palette entries of real images are randomly distributed therefore using this method it is never necessary to depart from the original colour too much. This avoids the problem of occasionally having to make large changes in colour which might indicate that a message has been hidden. Fridrich claims that his/her method of pseudo randomly changing the LSB of a pixel by locating the closest pixel colour in the palette rather than adjusting the palette as with EzStego produces approximately four times less distortion to the carrier image. Fridrich finds the distance between colours whereas EzStego orders the palette by luminance. This is the final steganography method to be encoded and evaluated. It is based on the method of Fridrich but instead of searching for the closest colour each time a bit is to be hidden in a pixel the closest colour to each colour in the palette with the opposite parity bit is initially chosen. This reduces the problem of having to search through the palette each time a bit is to be hidden. The pixels in which to hide the message are also pseudo randomly chosen in this study a technique which Fridrich also uses.

6.8 Cryptography – Knapsack

An encryption method will be investigated and will be provided as one of the final options for the user. The purpose here is not to use or develop a secure cryptographic method but to use a relatively simple method which contains a key in order to more randomly distribute the message over the image. Knapsack was the first algorithm for generalized public key encryption. Unfortunately it was found to be insecure.

The idea behind Knapsack is that, given a pile of items each having different weights it is possible to put some of them into a Knapsack so that the Knapsack weighs a given amount. Given a set of values M_1, M_2, M_3, ...M_n and a sum S the values of b_i are computed so that S = $b_1M_1 + b_2M_2 + b_3M_3 + ...b_nM_n$. The values of b_i can be either 0 or 1. 1 means that the value is in the sack 0 means that it is not.

This method has a public key and a private key. The private key is a super-increasing sequence of numbers. A series of bits related to the plaintext are compared with the key.
Values in the key which have a 1 opposite them are added to the sum S i.e. the total weight. A series of numbers generated in this manner builds up and this becomes the encrypted code.

A public key is also used. All of the values in the super-increasing sequence are multiplied by a number n. mod m. The modulus must be a number greater than the sum of all the values in the super-increasing sequence. n the multiplier should have no factors in common with m. The sequence of numbers produced is the public key.

6.9   How Steganography works

The best types of images to use are black and white greyscale or natural photographs with 24 bits per pixel which have been scanned in. The redundancy of the data helps to hide the presence of a secret message. A cover image should contain some randomness. It should contain some natural uncertainty or noise. Hiding information may introduce enough visible noise to raise suspicion. Therefore the carrier or cover image must be carefully selected. Once it has been used the image should not be used again and should be destroyed. A familiar image should not be used so it is better for the steganographer to create his / her own images. Some software displays the image before and after data is hidden. This will also be done here.

The user will be someone who is familiar with the process of information hiding and will have a knowledge of Information systems. Cryptography is recommended and will result in a more random looking message rather than a high degree of regularity. A cryptographic method will be included as an option prior to steganography.

The user should be able to select a plaintext message from a file, an image to be used as the carrier and then select a steganographic method which will hide the selected message in the selected carrier image. The user will then be able to save the stegoed image in another file. The user should also be provided with the option to encrypt the message prior to hiding it in the image. The user should be able to open an image file containing a stegoed image containing a message to be read and choose an appropriate method to unstego the message from the image. The user should then be provided with the hidden message. A graphical user interface will be provided for the user to select the appropriate files and methods.

The software will provide a GUI which will allow the user to select the file containing the message, the image in which to store the message and a file in which to store the stegoed image. The user will also be able to select the method for steganography and for encryption if desired.

7   The Steganographic System

Here we introduce the Steganographic Java Software Version 1.0 developed by Karen Bailey. The software is available free of charge for non-commercial research purposes. It can be downloaded from the following URL http://www.infm.ulst.ac.uk/~kevin/steganography.zip.

As Steganographic V.1.0 is written in Java. Any machine capable of running a Java VM is capable of running the software. The system was written in Java version 1.3.

The opening frame of the graphical user interface which is shown below contains a series of buttons one, to encrypt a message, one to decrypt a message, one for each of the seven steganography methods and one for each of the seven methods to reverse the steganography process and finally a Help button and an Exit button.

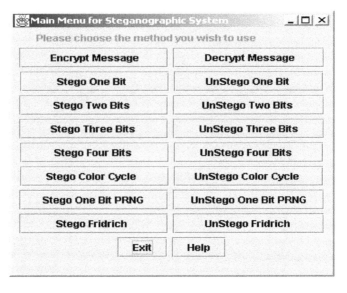

Figure 17: Main Menu for Steganographic System

7.1   Stegoing an Image

When for example Button1 (Sego One Bit) is pressed a message box which is shown below is displayed requesting that the user select a Gif image which contains 128 different colours in its palette.

Figure 18: Message Box asking user to select an image

This is the required image format for the method Stego One Bit due to the fact that this method may result in the formation of one new colour for each of the colours already in the palette. If the palette starts with 128 colours this allows for 128 additional or new colours to be produced. Method openGifFile is called to open a JFileChooser which allows the user to select a Gif image. The JFileChooser contains an ExtensionFilter object created from the ExtensionFilter class which allows only Gif files to be displayed in the JFileChooser. The JFileChooser is shown below. This immediately shows the user only Gif files from which he/she can select a suitable file containing an image. The directory and name of the file are returned from openGifFile to the ButtonHandler Actionperformed method.   If exit is pressed on the JfileChooser control goes back to the original GUI and the user can select any button to begin the process again.

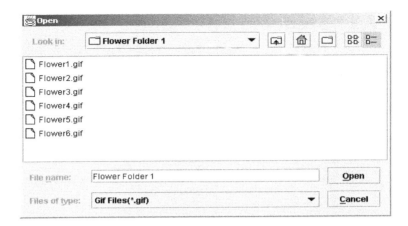

Figure 19: Selecting a Gif file/Image to be Stegoed

If a Gif file is chosen a ImageViewer object is created calling the ImageViewer class to display the image corresponding to the file name in a frame on the screen as shown below.

Figure 20: Displaying the Image to be Stegoed

A message box is then displayed asking the user to select a file containing a message to embed in the image. The message box is shown below. The openTextFile method is called to open a JFileChooser to select a text file.

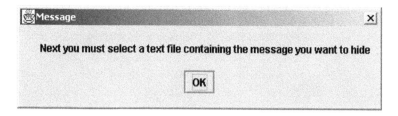

Figure 21: Message Box asking the user to select a text message

As before this JFileChooser contains an ExtensionFilter object and this time only text messages are displayed.

Figure 22: Selecting a message to be Stegoed into an Image

The directory and file name are returned to the actionPerformed method. As before if exit was pressed on the JFileChooser control returns to the GUI with the buttons. When a file containing a message has been chosen another message box is displayed containing the directory and file names of both the chosen image and the chosen message and asks the user to select the file in which the stegoed image is to be stored.

Figure 23: Message Box telling user the files they have chosen

The saveStegoGifFile method is called. This is very similar to the openGifFile method except that it is used to select the file in which the stegoed image will be saved.

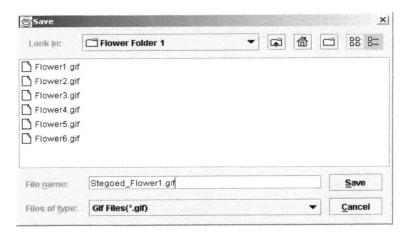

Figure 24: Choosing where to save the Stegoed Image

The actionPerformed method then creates an object of the class StegoedGifImage sending it the names of each of the three selected files and a flag. The flag corresponds to a particular steganographic method and is used later to determine the size of the message that can be saved in the selected image by a particular steganography method and which method to select to carry out the steganography. Finally a StegoedImageViewer object is created which displays the stegoed image in a frame on the screen for the user to see.

Figure 25: Displaying the Stegoed Image

Each of the buttons used to carry out steganography goes through this sequence of events.

7.2 Unstegoing an Image

If one of the buttons for unstegoing an image is chosen the following sequence of events occurs. A message box is displayed asking the user to select a file containing a stegoed Gif image to decode. The message box is shown below.

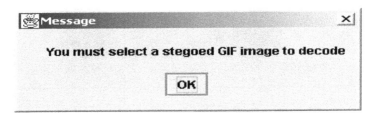

Figure 26: Message Box telling user to choose an Image to Unstego

Method openGifFile is called which is the same method used above to select a Gif file. It is called to open a JFileChooser and allow the user to select a file containing a Gif image. The directory and name of the file are returned to the ButtonHandler actionPerformed method.

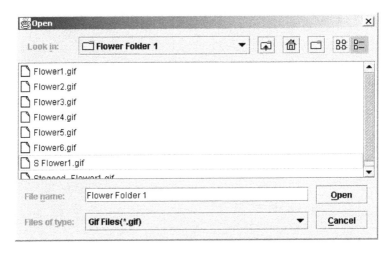

Figure 27: Choosing the Image to be Untegoed

A ImageViewer object is created displaying the stegoed image on the screen for the user to see.

Figure 28: Displaying the Image to be Unstegoed

An object of the UnStegoedGifImage is created which reads a message from the image, sending in gifFileName which is the name of the file in which the stegoed image is stored and a flag which determines the un stego method to be used. The unstego method un-stegoes the image and displays the message.

7.3   Encrypting a Message

If the Encrypt Message button is pressed a message box is displayed asking the user to select a file containing a message to encrypt. As before the openTextFile method allows the user to select a text file this time containing a message to be encrypted. A message box displays the directory and message file name and the user is then asked to select another text file in which to store the encrypted message. The saveEncryptedFile method is called and this will display a JFileChooser to allow the user to choose a file to save the encrypted message in. The knapSack method in the KnapSack class is then called sending it the message file and the file in which the encrypted message is to be stored and it carries out encryption on the message.

7.4   Decrypting a Message

If the Decrypt Message button is pressed a message is displayed asking the user to select a file contained the message to be decrypted. The openTextFile method is called as before to select the file containing the message, this time a message to be decrypted. The textFileName a string is returned. A message box then displays the name of the file containing the message to be decrypted. The knapSackDecrypt method is called in KnapSack and it is sent the name of the file and it returns a message in the form of a string. If no message was found a message box is displayed telling the user. If a message is found a MessageBox object is created which allows the message to be displayed on the screen in a Jframe.

7.5   Overview of the Classes

The following is a brief description of the classes used in the system.   The MenuBox class has already been described.

7.5.1 KnapSack Class

When the knapSack method is called a string array is created called message. The knapSack method contains an integer called maxStringSize. This integer contains a value which is the maximum length in characters that the message can be and relates to the average or typical amount of data an image can hold. The readMessage method is called in the MessageHandler class and is sent the textFileName and the maxStringSize. It returns the message from the file and stores it in the string array called message. Another string array called binaryString is created and it is eight times the size of the original message (8 bits per character). The convertMessageToBinary method is called which is in the CharacterBinaryConverter class sending it the string array called message and the maxStringSize integer. It returns the binaryString which is an array of binary values representing the message. The encryptKnapSack method is called and is sent the binaryString string array. This is the encryption method and it takes the binary values which relate to characters in the message and converts them into a series of positive integers. It returns an integer array called knappedNumbers containing the positive integers. This integer array was initialised at the start of the method to a value of 11000. This is because 8000 characters in maxStringSize could produce 64000 bits which can produce just under 11000 integer values using 6 bit chunks to produce an encrypted number. This method returns an integer array called knappedNumbers which is the result of the encryption process. The writeMessage method in the MessageHandler class is called sending it the encrypted message knappedNumbers and the name of the file into which it is to be saved called saveFileName. The encrypted message is therefore saved in a text file in the same way as unencrypted messages are saved in text files. This means that when a steganography method is chosen the message to be embedded in the image can either be an ordinary message from a text file or an encrypted message from a text file.

When binaryString is sent to the encryptKnapSack method an integer array is firstly created called knappedNumbers which is the same as the integer used in the knapSack method. Initially all the values in knappedNumbers are set to −1. As the Knapsack algorithm produces only positive integers the −1 values will be replaced by a set of positive integers. To carry out the encryption method a selection of integers are chosen. They are the public key and are used to produce a total integer value. The public key is usually about 250 items long however in this case it is 6. In blocks of six, each bit in the binaryString is examined in turn. If the bit has a value of 1it is assigned a number from the public key sequence of numbers. If the bit has a value of 0 no number is assigned to it and it does not contribute to the final total. When the 6 bit block has been examined the total value derived from adding the numbers is assigned to the array knappedNumbers. The next block of six bits is then examined and the number assigned to it is the next number in knappedNumbers array. The cycle goes on through all the bits in binaryString. An array of integer values called knappedNumbers has been produced and is returned to the knapsack method.

The knapSackDecrypt method can be called by selecting the Decrypt button on the GUI. This method is sent the textFileName. It contains an integer called maxStringSize in the same way that the encryption method contains an integer called maxStringSize. But this time it is larger and its size was chosen because the highest integer produced by encryptKnapSack will be three digits long and each integer will be separated by a ',' resulting in a maximum of 44000 individual character values 0 to 9 and a comma. A string array is created to hold the characters of the encrypted message and is called encryptedMessage. The message is read from the file and stored in encryptedMessage. It is read using the MessageHandler readMessage method which is sent the variables maxStringSize and textFileName. The decryptKnapSack method is called and sent the variables encryptedMessage and maxStringSize and the method returns the decrypted message stored in a string called decryptedTextMessage.

The method decryptKnapSack search's the encryptedMessage array building each distinct number by utilizing the fact that each distinct number e.g. 125 is separated by a comma. Each distinct number is stored in an array called arrayedKnappedNumbers so that calculations can be carried out on them. The calculation involves the use of the private key. A string called subString is produced by this calculation and it is made up of 1 and 0 bits representing the original message. This is done in the following way. An integer is selected from the array it is calculated back to its private key form. It is then compared with the superincreasing sequence of private key values. If the highest value in the key is less than the integer, it is subtracted from the integer and a 1 bit is added to the subString array. The integer value has now been reduced to a new value. If the highest value in the private key is greater than the integer a 0 bit is added to the array. The integer value is compared with the next highest number in the same way and so on. The subString's are added to the decryptedBinaryMessage string and this final string represents the message in binary form. A sequence of bits is added to the final string as follows 01000000. This does not represent any character used in this programme. The reason for doing this is that when the binary data is converted to characters by the convertBinaryToMessage method in the CharacterBinaryConverter class the convertBinaryToMessage method will come to a series of bits it does not recognize and will stop converting them. If this series of bits were not added the convertBinaryToMessage method would continue to look for bits and would eventually cause an Array Index Out of Bounds exception. The convertBinaryToMessage method returns a string called decryptedTextMessage. This is returned to the knapSackDecrypt method which returns decryptedTextMessage back to the actionPerformed method of the Buttonhandler class and the message is displayed on the screen.

7.5.2 StegoedGifImage Class

The constructor is used to control the process of steganography and the different steganographic methods. It starts by calling the loadImage method in the ImageDeconstructor class and sending it the gifFileName. The purpose of loadImage is to produce and return a 3D array representing the pixels and their colours in the image. The three dimensions are imagePixels[row][column][values for red, green, blue and alpha] from the image.

The maximum number of rows in the image represented by the integer MAXROWS and the maximum number of columns in the image represented by integer MAXCOLS are determined. A value is then determined for an integer called maxStringSize. The value that goes into this variable corresponds to the method used to carry out steganography and hence the type of image required for the method and the amount of data the image can hold. For example if the flag (a value sent as a parameter into this method) is equal to 2, this refers to the method stego2Bits. This method requires an image with a 64-colour palette. It involves storing 2 bits in each pixel in the image. Therefore the maxStringSize will be the number of pixels in the image divided by 4. Each character contains 8 bits and two bits can be stored in each pixel therefore the number of characters that can be stored in the image is the number of pixels divided by 8 and multiplied by 2. When the method to be used is selected a value for the flag (an integer) is allocated and the maxStringSize is then determined based on the flag value. This will tell us how much information can be stored in this image by this method. The masStringSize is used to create a string array called message of size maxStringSize –1 because of the value at 0 in the array. The readmessage method in FileIO is called and sent the maxstringSize and the textFileName. This method returns the string array called message. A new string array called binaryString is created based on the size of the image. The convertMessageToBinary method in the CharacterBinaryConverter class is called and sent the message string and the maxStringSize. This method is used to convert the message to its binary representation.

The method returns the binaryString. This method was also used for the encryption method explained above.

A method is now chosen to hide the binary data in the image. The method to be used is selected based again on the value in the flag. A three dimensional integer array is returned representing the stegoed image called stegoedImage. Most of the methods used for steganography are sent the parameters imagePixels, MAXROWS, MAXCOLS and binaryString. However two of the methods used require a series of random values produced by a pseudo random number generator. These random numbers are used to randomly choose positions of pixels in the image where data is to be stored. In previous methods data is stored in the first pixel first, then the second pixel second and so on. The size of the image is sent to the pseudo random number generator and the method sends back an integer array containing pseudo-random locations in which to store the message bits. Finally in this method a ImageBuilder object is created which saves the stegoed image in a file. The constructor is sent the stegoedImage 3D array, MAXROWS, MAXCOLS and the gifFileStoreName.

Following this method are a series of methods which carry out steganography on the chosen image.

stegotheImage1Bit firstly loops through each row and each column in the 3D array imagePixels until all the bits to be hidden in the image have been hidden. Each character is extracted from the binary string and is stored in a character called binaryValue. If the character equals 1 and the least significant bit in the blue value of the current pixel is 0, 1 is added to it. If the character equals 0 and the least significant bit in the blue value of the current pixel is 1, 1 is subtracted from it. The least significant bit of the blue colours is determined using a Modula function. Otherwise the pixel is left alone. The method moves on to the next bit in the binaryString and the next pixel. If the pixels are left alone then no new colour is created in the palette. If a change is made in a pixel this creates a new colour. The adjusted (stegoed) imagePixels array is returned to the stegoBits method.

Using this method a given colour can become 2 other colours, hence a 128 colour palette should be used to start with.

The stegoTheImage2Bits method is very similar to stegoTheImage1Bit except that this time two bits are hidden in the pixel. The first bit is hidden in the least significant bit in the same way as stegoTheImage1Bit but the second bit is hidden in the second least significant bit. In order to do this a variable called secondBit is created. A bitwise AND operation is carried out on the pixel value to block out all the other bits except the bit representing 2. This time if the character equals 1 and the second least significant bit in the blue value of the current pixel is 0, 2 is added. If the character equals 0 and the second least significant bit in the blue value of the current pixel is 1, 2 is subtracted. Using this method a given colour can become 4 other colours, hence a 64 colour palette should be used to start with.

In the method stegoTheImage3Bits the same process as above is carried out except that this time three bits are hidden in each pixel. Using this method a given colour can become 8 other colours, hence a 32 colour palette should be used to start with. and in the stegoTheImage4Bits method 4 bits are hidden in each pixel. Using this method a given colour can become 16 other colours, hence a 16 colour palette should be used to start with. In each of these four methods bits are hidden in the least significant bits of the blue value. There is no particular reason for this it could have been any of the three colours. The human eye is most sensitive to green and therefore it was not selected.

In the method stegoTheImageColorCycle a similar process is carried out except that this time instead of the least significant bits of the blue value always being used to store the message the least significant bit of alternating colours are used going from red to green to blue and back to red skipping the alpha value. The alpha value is skipped because it is the transparency value and it would look odd if this value differed over the surface of the image.

stegoTheImage1BitPRNG is a method in which the binary bits are hidden in the least significant bit of the blue colour of pixels whose positions coincide with the positions stored in an array of pseudo randomly generated pixel positions. The array position initially comprises a single value which must be reduced to a pair of row and column coordinates. The method loops through the dataPositions array. This array is sent in when the method is called and it consists of the array of pseudo randomly generated numbers corresponding to the position of pixels in the image. The method extracts from the array a pseudo randomly generated value corresponding to the position of a pixel in the image. It then iteratively subtracts the width of the image (MAXCOLS) from the array value, incrementing the row value (tempROWS) as it goes. It is counting through the rows in the image until it finds the position corresponding to the number in the array. It does this until the array value (dataPositions[counter]) is less than the width of the image which allows the column value (tempCOLS) where the pixel is located to be determined. The row value and the column value are recorded and the pixel in which to store the data can now be located in the same way as before. 1 is subtracted from the final column value as the image starts from 0,0 but the pixel position values in the array start from 1.

The method stegoTheImageFridrich works in a different way. Like the method by Fridrich described in the introduction this method involves replacing the pixel colour with another pixel in the palette which is the shortest distance from the pixel colour. First of all one occurance of each pixel is put into a 2D array called imageValuesTable. The first four positions in column 0 are set to the red, green, blue and parity values of pixel 0, 0 in imagePixels. coloursFound is an integer variable representing the number of different colours found to date in imagePixels. To find the unique colurs the method cycles through every position in imagePixels and checks to see if its RGB value is already stored in the imageValuesTable array. If it is the method moves on to the next value in imagePixels. If it is not stored it is added to the imageValuesTable array along with its parity value. A check is carried out on the values in imageValuesTable to determine if the image is suitable for this steganography method. The image must have different parity values in its pixels. If all the parity values in the pixels are the same the image cannot be used. Each value in imageValuesTable is paired with its closest colour in the table by distance which has a different parity. To do this the current position (tablePosition) is checked against every other position in the table by cycling through the table (increment tempRow) calculating the distance between the positions and storing the closest other colour with a different parity in a set of temporary variables. After comparing every colour against the current colour (tablePosition) the closest colour with a different parity should be in the temporary variables. Finally the method cycles through the image and the binaryString. For each pixel whose parity equals the corresponding binary value the pixel is left alone. But for each pixel whose parity does not equal the corresponding binary value it is replaced with the closest colour which has a different parity found in the imageValuesTable array. The pixels and binaryValues under comparison are matched using a pseudo random number generator in the same way as in method stego1BitPRNG.

7.5.3 UnStegoedGifImage Class

.When an object of UnSteggoGifImage is created the loadImage method in ImageDeconstructor class is called sending it the gifFileName and it returns a 3D integer array called unStegoImage. The height and width of the image are determined and the size put into integer variables MAXROWS and MAXCOLS. The flag which is sent in as a parameter to unStegoBits determines the un stego method to be called. The appropriate method is called sending it the 3D array unStegoImage, MAXROWS and MAXCOLS. Each un-stego method returns a string called hiddenMessage which contains the message read from the stegoed image. For two of the methods unStegoTheImage1BitPRNG   and unStegoTheImageFridrich an extra parameter is required called dataPositions. dataPositions is an integer array which is the size of the number of pixels in the image. It is returned from the PRNG method in the PRNGenerator class and is a pseudo random array of integers representing positions of pixels in the image. It is sent to the un stego method to determine the order in which the least significant bit of the pixels or the parity bit should be read. Obviously there is an un stego method for each of the stego methods in the system and each method operates by generally reversing the stego process and reading the least significant or parity bits back out of the image, reassembling them and converting them back to a string which is the message.

If there is nothing in the string a message is displayed which states "No message was found in the chosen image Please check that you have chosen a stegoed image and the correct unStego method."

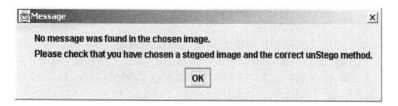

Figure 29: Message Box telling user no message was found in the chosen Image

Otherwise a MessageBox object is created and the message is displayed in a frame on the screen. Sometimes the unStego method will find some letters even if no message was embedded in the first place. After the unstegoed message has been displayed a system message "Message Decoded" is displayed so that the user will be aware that the process is finished.

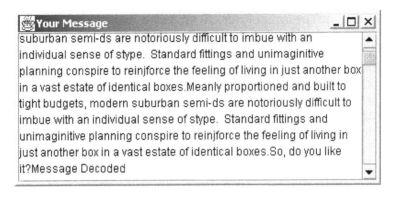

Figure 30: The Unstegoed/extracted message

The first un-stego method in the class is unStegoTheImage1Bit. This method takes in the 3D array representing the stegoed image. It then loops through the image extracting the least significant bit of the blue value in each pixel using a Modula function. It appends that bit to a string representing the bits called extractedBinaryMessage. The string representing the bits in the column lineofExtractedBinaryMessage is added to the overall string representing the bits called extractedBinaryMessage. This process of reading a row at a time improves performance significantly rather than adding bits directly on to one string. The extractedBinaryMessage string is then sent to the convertBinaryToMessage method in the CharacterBinaryConverter class and the extractedMessage string is returned containing the message read from the image.

UnStegoTheImage2Bits works in much the same way as unStegoTheImage1Bit except that this time it also extracts the second last bit of the blue value in each pixel using the bitwise AND function and appends that bit to the string representing the bits called extractedBinaryMessage. unStegoTheImage3Bits and unStegoTheImage4Bits work in the same way except that three or four bits are extracted instead of two.

The method unStegoTheImageColorCycle is again a similar method to the above four but this time the least significant bit of alternate colours is read from the image. The method cycles through the colours starting with red, and then going to green and then blue. It then goes back to red. The unStegoTheImage1BitPRNG method must firstly determine the pseudo randomly generated array of numbers. As before this is based on a key value. When running this method from the GUI the user will be asked for the key. The pseudo random array of numbers is generated in the same way as it was when the message was embedded in the image in the method stegoTheImage1BitPRNG. As before the numbers must be converted to column and row values to determine the location of the pixels to be examined. The least significant bit of these pixels are read and added to lineOfExtractedBinaryMessage.

Finally this class contains a method called unStegoTheImageFridrich. As before this method begins with determining the location of the pixels in the image by determining the row and column position corresponding to the pseudo randomly generated numbers. The parity bit is determined and attached onto lineOfExtractedBinaryMessage which is appended to extractedBinaryMessage in blocks of 100 characters for more efficient memory handling.

In each of these methods the extractedMessage is returned to unStegoBits.

7.5.4   ImageDeconstructor Class

In the method loadImage firstly a null image is created called img. While the image is null, the getDefaultToolkit() method in the Toolkit class calls the getImage method sending it the gifFileName. This method returns an object of type Toolkit called img which contains information about the environment in which the application is running including the screen size in pixels. A Button object is created to use as a parameter which is sent to the constructor for MediaTracker. A MediaTracker object is created called tracker to track the status of the image. tracker calls its addImage method sending it the image img. This adds the image and the ID to the tracker. Another method is called by the tracker object called waitForID. The purpose of this method is to start loading all the images tracked by this mediaTracker which have a particular identifier. Exception handling is carried out here therefore after img has been initialized as a null image the next block of code described above is in a try block. An exception is caught with a catch block and an error message is displayed. An object called observer is created from class IObserver. This object allows the use of methods getWidth and getHeight for the image which return the width and height of the image in pixels. The width and height and the Image img are then sent to the getImagePixels method returning a three dimensional array representing the imagePixels which are then returned to the StegoedGifImage class. The three dimensions are imagePixels[row][column][values for red, green, blue and alpha] from the image.

The Image object img, the width and the height are sent to the getImagePixels method. This method starts by calling the getPixels method sending it the same information (img, the width and the height). A one-dimensional array of integers called rawPixels is initialized. Its size is the width multiplied by the height of the image. A PixelGrabber object is then created. The object called pg grabs a rectangular section of pixels from the image and puts them into an array. Information including the width, height, the img and rawPixels are sent to the constructor to produce the pg object. The grabPixels method then requests that the Image start delivering pixels and waits for all of the pixels in the rectangle of interest to be delivered. An exception is caught if pixels are not retrieved. The rawPixels are returned to the getImagePixels method. The rawPixels data is a series of 32 bit values representing red, green, blue and alpha values for each pixel in the image.

Control now returns to the getImagePixels method. A new two-dimensional integer array is initialized called rgbPixels. Its size is the length of rawPixels, in other words the number of pixels in the image and 4 representing the red, green, blue and alpha values. Each of the 32 bit values in rawPixels is separated out into four 8-bit values for each pixel. The four 8 bit values are the values for red, green and blue and alpha. The red, green, blue and alpha values are positioned in the array with red in the first position, position 0, green in position 1, blue in position 2 and alpha in position 3. A new three-dimensional array called imagePixels is then initialized to contain values for height, width and 4 (the RGBA values). The data is taken from rgbPixels and entered into the new array so that it is arranged in rows and columns. The width of the image represents the number of columns and the height the number of rows. The 3D array is 4 positions deep to represent the RGBA values at the corresponding pixel coordinate. The 3D array imagePixels is returned to the StegoedGifImage class.

7.5.5 CharacterBinaryConverter Class

The first method in this class is convertMessageToBinary. The purpose of this method is to convert the message to be stegoed, which is an array of strings into a different array of strings which contains a binary representation of that message. The method first declares a string array called binaryString which has a string position for each pixel in the image the message will be hidden in. Its size is based on the parameter maxStringSize which represents the maximum possible size of the message string. The first problem here is that the message is in a string array and the switch statement which is used here can only evaluate characters. The string array is converted to a string. A character array is created one character long. Each character is extracted one at a time from the string and put into the character array. For each character in the character array the switch statement evaluates its value and converts it into a binary string representation of that value. It uses a method called converter which appends the binary string representation of that value to a string array called binaryString and returns binaryString. The binaryValue which is 8 bits in the form of a string is subdivided into each of its bits which are individually added to binaryString. When the character in the array has been converted to its binary form the next character is extracted from the string and so on. Each case statement calls the converter method sending it binaryString, mainCounter, and the binary value e.g."01000011". mainCounter is counting the number of bits in the message. binaryString is then returned to the method that called convertMessageToBinary.

The third method in this class is convertBinaryToMessage and it reverses the process carried out in the method convertMessageToBinary. This method loops through the string representing the binary bits in blocks of 8 passing the blocks to an if statement which converts them into text characters and appends the character to a string representing the extracted message. The method firstly steps through the string representing the binary bits in blocks of 8. It then evaluates the string representing a block of 8 bits and converts it to an appropriate character. The character is appended on to a string representing the unstegoed message. This process is repeated until a block is found which does not correspond to a known character. This is used to stop the method trying to read through a series of bits which are for example extracted from an unstegoed image or an image embedded by a different steganography method. The method compareTo is used here. If the block of 8 bits is the same as the value sent to the method in brackets a 0 is returned. Each time a character is found the position in the binary string is incremented by 8 bits. The extractedMessage string is retuned to the method which called convertBinaryToMessage.

7.5.6   MessageHandler Class

The messageIO class contains a readMessage method and a writeMessage method. Its purpose is to read messages from files or write message to files. readMessage takes in a parameter called maxStringSize. This determines the length of the message that can be read in i.e. the length of the message that can be stored in the particular image. A string array is created to hold the message. Its length is determined by maxStringSize. The method also takes in the name of the file containing the message . A FileReader is created and sent the file name. A BufferedReader is also created. Each line is read from the file while there is still something contained in the file. The file is then closed. This method contains exception handling. The length of the message is then determined. If the message from the file is smaller than maxStringSize the method copies the message from the file into the message array. If the message is too long a message box is displayed to tell the user that the message is too long for the image and that it will be truncated to fit into the image. Finally the message is returned to the method that called readMessage. The only time in this system that a message is written to a file is when a message has been encrypted. The writeMessage method takes in int [] knappedNumbers and String saveFileName as parameters. The knappedNumbers contains the numbers produced by the Knapsack algorithm. saveFileName is the file into which the message is to be stored. A FileWriter is created and sent the file name. A BufferedWriter is also created and a PrintWriter to write the knappedNumbers to a file. The knappedNumbers are written out to a file and the file is closed. Exception handlers are also contained in this method.

7.5.7 ImageBuilder Class

The purpose of this class is to link up with the GifEncoder class to save the stegoed image in a file. The ImageBuilder constructor takes in the parameters int[][][] imagePixels, int MAXROWS, int MAXCOLS, String ImageBuilderName. This includes the 3D array representing the pixels of the image, the number of columns and number of rows in the image and the file name into which the image is to be saved. First of all the constructor takes the 3D array representing the image to be saved and creates a one-dimensional array which will hold the reassembled 32 bit raw pixel values from the 3D array. It does this by looping through the rows and columns of the 3D array and combining the RGBA values back together into their correct order. The method then creates an Image object called finalImage from the 1D array of 32 bit raw pixel values. The saveFile method is called sending it finalImage and ImageBuilderName. This method takes the image to be saved and writes it to a gif image file using the GIFEncoder provided. Exceptions such as finding the file and writing to the file are caught.

7.5.8 PRNGenerator Class

The purpose of this class is to produce a pseudo random non-repeating sequence of numbers based on the number of pixels in the image and a unique key. The user uses a key to start the process of generating the numbers. An integer representing the size of the picture called pictureSize is taken in as a parameter. First of all int i is determined. i is a non factor of the pictureSize. A method called findNonFactors is used to do this. This is done by determining which numbers divide evenly into the picture size, starting with 2. If for example 2 does not divide in evenly it is not a factor and it is returned. If it does it is a factor and three is tested and so on. The step size is then determined. It is the pictureSize divided by i. This is the size of the step the system will jump to the next pseudo random number. A one dimensional integer array called dataPositions is created in which to hold the pseudo random numbers. The pictureSize and stepSize should have no factors in common. This is so that as the number generator loops through the image it wont choose the same number twice. A method called findFactors is used to determine if they have factors in common.

A new integer array called stepSizeFactors is created and initialized to the same size as   stepSize. The values in it are all set to 0. An integer counter is created and initialized to 2. The counter value 2 is Modula-ed with stepSize. If it is equal to 0 counter is added to the stepSizeFactors array i.e it is a factor. The for loop increases counter by one and tests it again and so on until it reaches the end of the loop i.e. stepsize. A test is then carried out to determine if the values in stepSizeFactors are factors of pictureSize using a Modula function. If they are a flag is returned. If the flag shows that stepSize is a factor of pictureSize. StepSize is increased by 1. This test is continued until stepsize is not a factor of pictureSize. The user is then asked to enter a key, any positive integer value that is not 0. The key is entered as a string and is then converted to an integer. The key is the starting position in the image from which the pseudo random numbers are generated. The key would be the first number. It is called integer pos. The second number is the key plus the stepSize. The third number is the key plus the stepSize multiplied by 2 and so on until every position in the image is accounted for. The calculation is pos = key + (stepSize * counter) and counter is an increasing integer staring with 0. If pos becomes greater than the pictureSize it is Modula-ed with the pictureSize and the remainder is pos. In this way the method cycles through the image several times. pos is placed in dataPositions adding 1 to it in case pos has a value of 0. The pseudo randomly generated numbers/positions are stored in dataPositions and then the process has finished the dataPositions array is returned.

8 Conclusion

The object of steganography is to send a message through some innocuous carrier to a receiver while preventing anyone else from knowing that a message is being sent. The carrier can be one of several forms of digital media however the most common type of carrier used is an image. The image should not attract any attention as a carrier of a message and should look as close as possible to an ordinary image by the human senses. Different properties of the image can be manipulated in order to store the message including colour and luminescence.

When images are used as the carrier in steganography they are generally manipulated by changing one or more of the bits of the byte or bytes that make up the pixels of an image. The least significant bit (LSB) of a byte may be used to encode the bits of the message. Messages characters can be converted to bytes in binary form and then each bit of this binary list of bytes can be stored a bit at a time in a series of pixels. These LSBs can then be read by the recipient of the stegoed image and put together as bytes in order to reproduce the hidden message. This process will not noticeable alter the visual appearance of a colour. The second third fourth etc least significant bits can be used to store data. Changing a more significant bit may cause a proportionately greater change in the visual appearance of a colour

Other aspects of the image can be manipulated in order to store data. The texture of some background surfaces in the image can be manipulated. The message may be spread evenly over the entire image or may be introduced into areas where it may be difficult to detect a small change such as an area of high frequency. A message could be repeated over the image multiple times in a type of pattern. In this way if any part of the image is lost or cropped the message can still be read. A pseudo random number generator could be used to choose random pixels or areas in which to embed the message.

There are two ways of hiding messages in palette-based images: embedding the message in the palette or embedding the message into the image pixels. Embedding into an image will result in the production of new colours. The palette must be able to cope with these new colours. If the palette is created which contains 128 colours this will allow for the creation of 1 new colour for every existing colour in the palette. The only restriction is then the size of the image. If two bits in the image are to be manipulated then the string number of colours in the palette must be reduced even further to 64 and so on for increased storage of data.

Another possibility is to determine the closest colour by distance with a different parity bit to all the colours in the palette. When a colour is replaced by its closest colour with the correct parity bit is will be relatively close to the original colour. An advantage of this method is also that it results in no changes to the palette itself. Another way of storing a message is to permute the palette instead of the colours of the image using for example a process called Gifshuffle. This involves moving the colours in the palette into a very specific order relating to the message to be stored. Bits of information can also be inserted into coefficients of image transforms such as Fourier Transform or Discrete Cosine Transform. Adaptive steganography adapts the message embedding technique to the actual content and features of the image for example avoiding areas of uniform colour.

A suitable image and in the case of palette based images a suitable palette needs to be chosen for steganography. The best types of images to use are black and white greyscale or natural photographs with 24 bit per pixel which have been scanned in. The cover image should contain some noise. Once it has been used the image should not be used again and should be destroyed.

Some methods investigated in this study included:_Hide and Seek, EzStego, a method by the author Fridrich, S-Tools, StegoDos, White Noise Storm, Gifshuffle, Mandelsteg, Stealth and Steganos. There are many others. Steganalysis is the art of discovering a message.

Breaking a steganographic system involves detecting that steganography has been used and reading the embedded message and proving that the message has been embedded to third parties. Steganalysis methods are also used by the steganographer in order to determine whether a message is secure and consequently whether a steganographic process has been successful.

Detection involves observing relationships between combinations of cover, message, stego-media and steganography tools. This can be achieved by passive observation of patterns or unusual exaggerated noise and visual corruption. The patterns visible to the human eye could broadcast the existence of a message and point to signatures of certain methods or tools used. If numerous comparisons can be made between the cover images and the stego-images patterns can begin to emerge. Some of the methods of carrying out steganography produce characteristics that act as signatures for that steganography method. Detection might involve looking at areas in the image where colour does not flow well from one area to another. The attacker should obviously not be familiar with the cover image.

Statistical attacks can be carried out using automated methods. Automation can be used to investigate pixel neighbourhoods and determining if an outstanding pixel is common to the image, follows some sort of pattern or resembles noise. A knowledge base of predictable patterns can be compiled and this can assist in automating the detection process. A person wishing to detect someone else's stegoed images may analyse the type of equipment being used to create the image such as a scanner or digital camera. In order to prevent detection steganographic keys can be used. A steganographic key controls embedding and extracting of the message. The key could scatter the message randomly over the carrier.

Watermarking is the process of hiding information in a carrier in order to protect text, music, films and art. Generally information is hidden about the carrier itself providing further information about the image. The message can also be encrypted before it is hidden in the image so that if it is found it won't necessarily be readable and also it randomises the message over the image.

References

Beck Alan, Fractal Tutorials, 2000,
http://library.thinkquest.org/12740/netscape/discover

Brown A., S-Tools for Windows, Shareware, 1994.
ftp://idea.sec.dsi.unimi.it/pub/security/crypt/code/s-tools3.zip(version   3),
ftp://idea.sec.dsi.unimi.it/pub/security/crypt/code/s-tools4.zip(version 4)

Brown W., Shepherd B.J., Graphics File Formats:
Reference and Guide. Manning Publications Greenwich,
CT, 1995.

Cha S. D., G. H. Park, H. K. Lee, A Solution to the Image
Downgrading Problem, ACSAC, pp. 108-112, 1995.

Cole E., Steganography Information System Security
paper, George Mason University, 1997

Cox I., J. Kilian, T. Shamoon, T. Leighton, A Secure
Robust Watermark for Multimedia, Information Hiding:
First International Workshop Proceedings, Cambridge, UK,
Lecture Notes in Computer Science vol. 1174, Berlin,
Heidelberg, New York, Springer-Verlag, 1996.

Day Bill and Knudsen Jonathan, Image Processing with
Java 2D www.javaworld.com/javaworld/jw-09-1998/jw-09-media_p.html, Aug. 1998.

Efford, Nick, Digital Image Processing a Practical
Introduction using Java, Addison-Wesley, 2000.

Flickner M., Query by Image and Video Content: The
QBIC System IEEE Computer 28 (9): 23-32, 1995.

Frankel C., M.J. Swain, Vathitsos Webseer – An Image
Search Engine for the World Wide Web, University of
Chicago Computer Science Department, Technical Report
96-14, 1996.

Fridrich Jiri, A New Steganographic Method for Palette-Based Images. Center for Intelligent Systems, SUNY Binghamton, Binghamton, New York. IS&T's PICS Conference. pp285-289, 1999.

Fridrich Jiri, Rui Du, Secure Steganographic Methods for Palette Images. Center for Intelligent Systems, Dept. of SS&IE, SUNY Binghamton, Binghamton, New York. Information Hiding, Third International Workshop, IH'99 Dresden Germany, September / October Proceedings, Computer Science 1768. pp. 47-60, 2000.

Goldreich Oded, Foundations of Cryptography, Basic Tools, Cambridge University Press, 2001

Grhul D., W. Bender, Information Hiding to Foil the Casual Counterfeiter, Information Hiding, Second International Workshop, IH'98 Portland, Oregon, USA, Proceedings, Computer Science 1525. pp. 1-15, April 1998.

Hansmann F. Steganos. Deus Ex Machina Communications. http://www.steganography.com 1996

Hastur, H: Mandelsteg, ftp://ftp.csua.berkeley.edu/pub/cypherpunks/steganograp hy, 1998

Heckbert Paul, Colour Image Quantization for Frame Buffer Display. In Proceedings of SIGGRAPH 82, 1982.

Hellman M.E., The Mathematics of Public Key Cryptography, Scientific American vol. 241, n. 8 Aug 1979, pp.146-157

Hsieh Ing-Sheen and Kuo-Chin Fan, An Adaptive Clustering Algorithm for Colour Quantization, Science Direct, Elsevier Science, vol. 21, n. 4, April 2000, pp. 337-346.

Johnson Neil F., Sushil Jajodia, Steganalysis of Images Created Using Current Steganography Software, Centre for Secure Information Systems, George Mason University, Fairfax, Virginia, Information Hiding, Second

International Workshop, IH'98 Portland, Oregon, USA, Proceedings, Computer Science 1525. pp. 273-289, April 1998.

a. Johnson Neil F. An Introduction to Watermark Recovery from Images, http://www.jjtc.com/pub/nfjidr99.pdf Centre for Secure Information Systems, George Mason University, proceedings of the SANS Intrusion, Detection and Resonse Confernece, San Diego, February 1999

Johnson Neil, F. Z. Duric, S. Jajodia, A Role of Digital Watermarking in Electronic Commerce, accepted for publication by the ACM, 1999.

Johnson Neil F., Zoran Duric, Sushil Jajodia, Information Hiding, Steganography and Watermarking - Attacks and Countermeasures, Kluwer Academic Publishers, 2001.

Kahn D. The Codebreakers: The Story of Secret Writing. New York, Macmillan Publishing Co., 1967.

Kurak C., J. McHugh, A Cautionary Note on Image Downgrading, IEEE Eight Annual Computer Security Applications Conference, pp. 153-159, 1992.

Kwan Matthew, How GifShuffle Works, 1998. http://www.darkside.com.au/gifshuffle/description.html

Lai X. On the Design and Security of Block Ciphers ETH Series in Information Processing v. 1 Konstanz:Hartung-Gorre Verlag 1992

Lemstrom K. and P. Franti, N-Candidate Methods for Location Invariant Dithering of Colour Images, Science Direct, Elsevier Science, vol. 18, n. 6-7, May 2000, pp. 493-500.

Machado, R. EzStego, Stego Online, Stego, http://www.stego.com, 1996

Maroney Colin, HideSeek v5.0, www.rugeley.demon.co.uk/security/hdsk50.zip

Mel H.X. and Doris Baker, Cryptography Decrypted, Addison-Wesley, 2001

Merkle R.C. and M. Hellman, Hiding Information and Signatures in Trap Door Knapsacks, IEEE Transactions on Information Theory, v.24, n. 5. Sept. 1978 pp. 525-530

Murray James D., William van Ryper, Encyclopedia of Graphics File Formats, Second Edition, O'Reilly and Associates Inc., 1996

Nelson Mark, The Data Compression Book, M&T Books, 1992

Niblack W., The QBIC Project: Querying Images by Content using Colour, Texture and Shape Storage and Retrieval for Image and Video Databases SPIE vol. 1908 February 1993.

NIST, National Institute of Standards and Technology NIST FIPS PUB 186, Digital Signature Standard, U.S. Department of Commerce, May 1994

Oakes Scott, Java Security, Second Edition, O'Reilly and Associates Inc, 2001

Pfitzmann Birgit, Information Hiding Terminology Collected by Birgit Pfitzmann, Information Hiding, First International Workshop, Cambridge, UK, Proceedings, Computer Science 1174. pp. 347-350, May / June 1996.

Repp, Heinz., Hide4PGP,version 1 and 2 http://www.rugeley.demon.co.uk/security/hide4pgp.zip

Ritter Terry, Learning about Cryptography, September 2002, http://www.ciphersbyritter.com/LEARNING.HTM

Rivest R. L., A. Shamir and L.M. Adleman, A Method for Obtaining Digital Signatures and Public key Cryptosystems, Coomunicatiosn of the ACM, vol. 21, no. 2, Feb. 1978, pp. 120-126.

Rosenfeld A., Models: The Graphics Vision Interface, edited by T.L. Kunii, Visual Computing, Springer, Tokyo, pp.21-23, 1992

Sanders D., Stegodetect. Steganography Detection Tool, 1997.

Schneier Bruce, Applied Cryptography, Second Edition, John Wiley & Sons, 1996

Smith Richard E. Internet Cryptography, Addison-Wesley 1997

Stevens Roger T., Graphics Programming with Java, Second Edition, Charles River Media Inc. Rockland Massachusetts, 1999.

Wayner Peter, Disappearing Cryptography, Information Hiding: Steganography and Watermarking, 2nd Edition, Morgan Kaufmann Publishers, 2002.

Westfield Andreas and Andreas Pfitzmann, Attacks on Steganographic Systems Breaking the Steganography Utilities EzStego, Jsteg, Steganos and S-Tools and Some Lessons Learned. Dresden University of Technology, Department of Computer Science, Information Hiding, Third International Workshop, IH'99 Dresden Germany, September / October Proceedings, Coputer Science 1768. pp. 61- 76, 1999.

Wohlgemuth Sven, IT-Security: Theory and Practice. Steganography and Watermarking, IIG Telematics WS, January 8, 2002.
http://www.informatik.uni-freiburg.de/~softech/teaching/ws01/itsec

Zollner J., H. Federrath, H. Klimant, A. Pfitzmann, R. Piotraschke, A. Westfeld, G. Wicke, G. Wolf, Modelling the Security of Steganographic Systems, Information Hiding, Second International Workshop, IH'98 Portland, Oregon, USA, Proceedings, Computer Science 1525. pp. 344-354, April 1998.

www.ingramcontent.com/pod-product-compliance
Lightning Source LLC
Chambersburg PA
CBHW071549080326
40690CB00056B/1614